MAGIC TOTEM

COLORING BOOK

NADIYA VASILKOVA

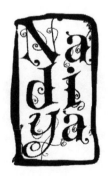

ISBN: 1532931875
ISBN-13: 978-1532931871

ABOUT AUTOR

I live in the Altai Mountains. This is a very beautiful place that many consider mystical. There people still believe in spirits and religion are shamanism. Altai inspires and gives me ideas for creativity.

I hand-draw the picture in black ink. My paintings are made up of many points, sometimes I use lines and fills. So, I am long enough drawing every picture.

I create images of spirits, totems, fairytale animals, so they are not realistic, and are filled with patterns. But for me very important to my images-spirits "looked" at the viewer. All life in his eyes.

I had a come a long way to my drawing style. I received his art education at the University. Creating a book one is my professions. I have worked with publishers and printing houses as an illustrator and designer. For a long time I taught at the University of Arts. I was recognized in the professional community of designers.

But some time ago, my family moved from a big city to the mountains, and I gave all my time to creativity.

Now many of my paintings have become popular all over the world, and I realized that it was time to publish my own book. I dream that my creative philosophy had followers. The main thing for me in art, this energy contact the artist and the viewer. In this coloring book, we will work with you. I will give you ideas and outlines, and you will fill them with color.

And it is unimportant near or far we are from each other, we all share a love for drawing.

I wish you good spirits while drawing.

Sincerely, Nadiya Vasilkova.

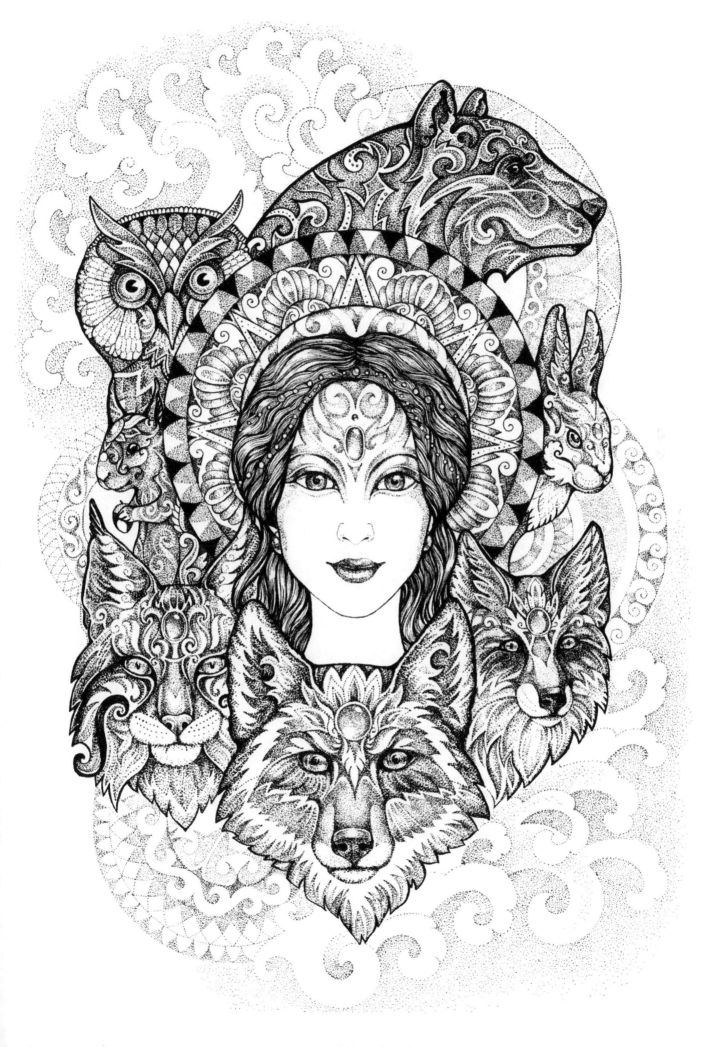

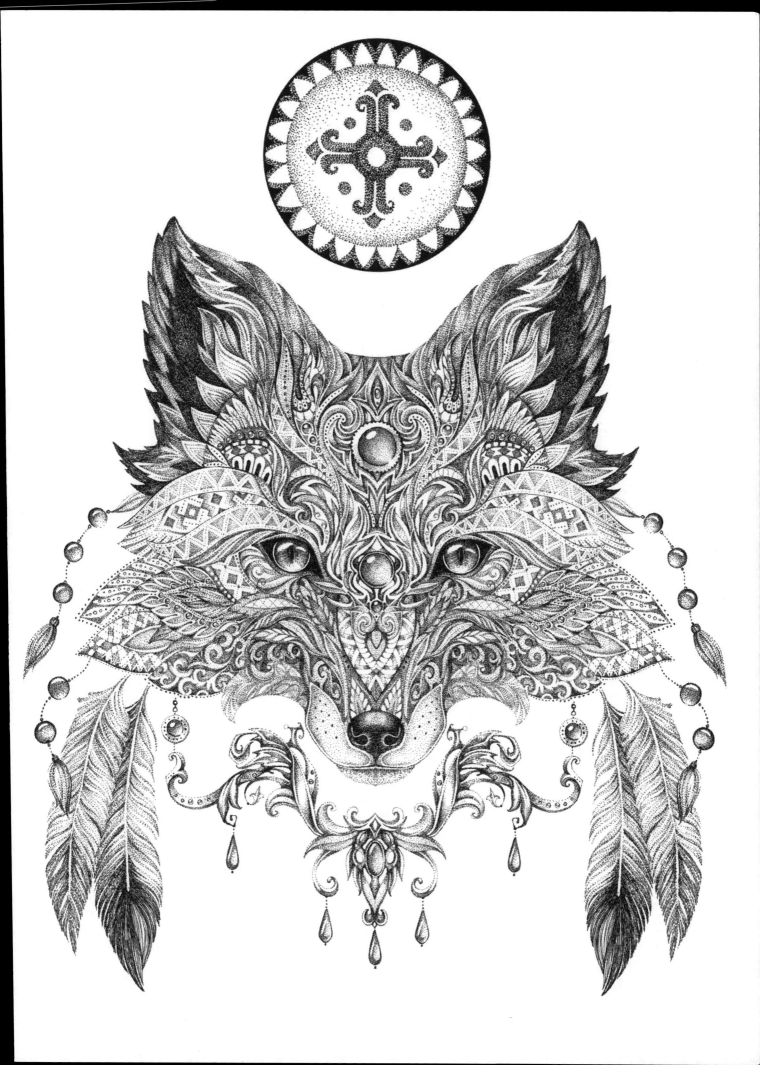

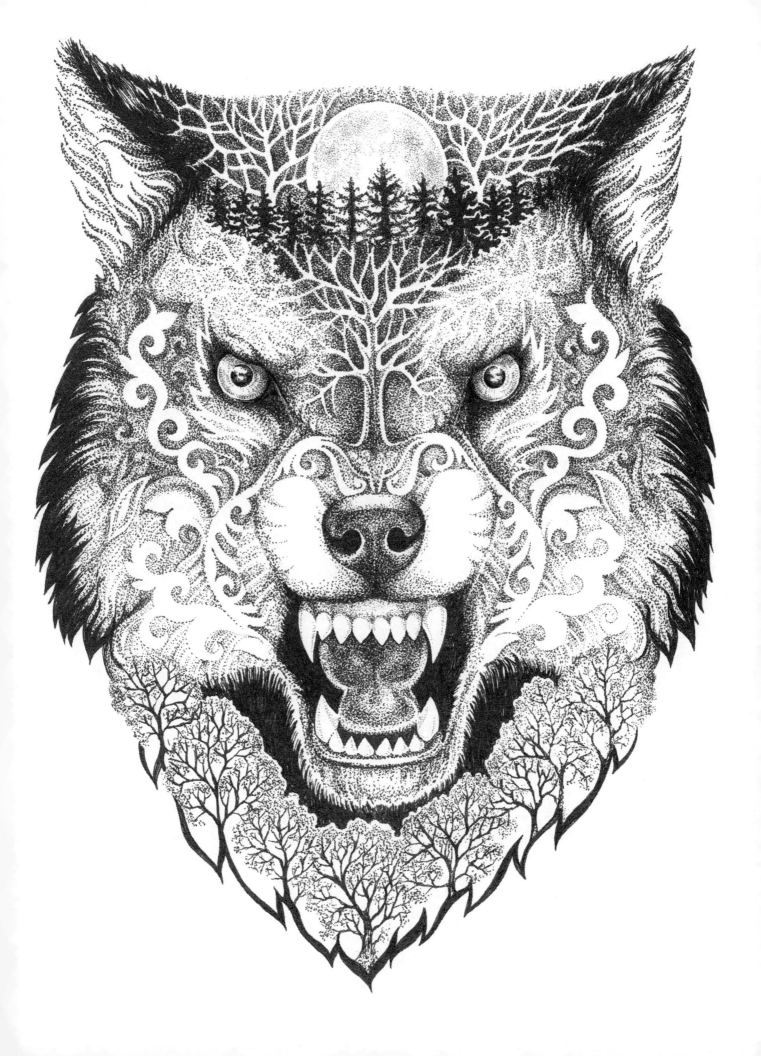

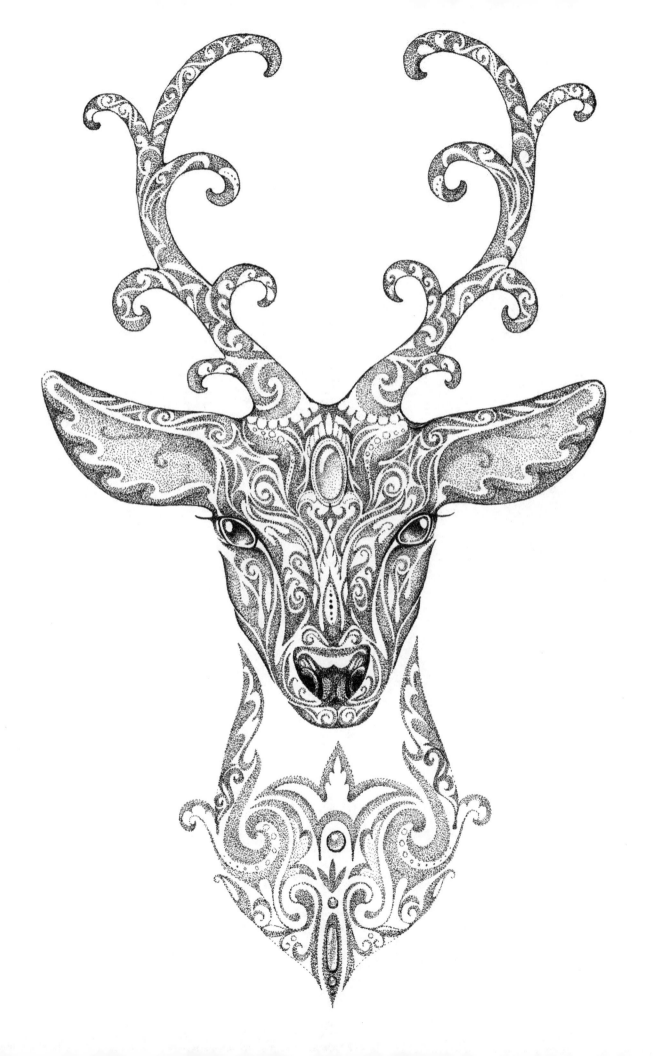

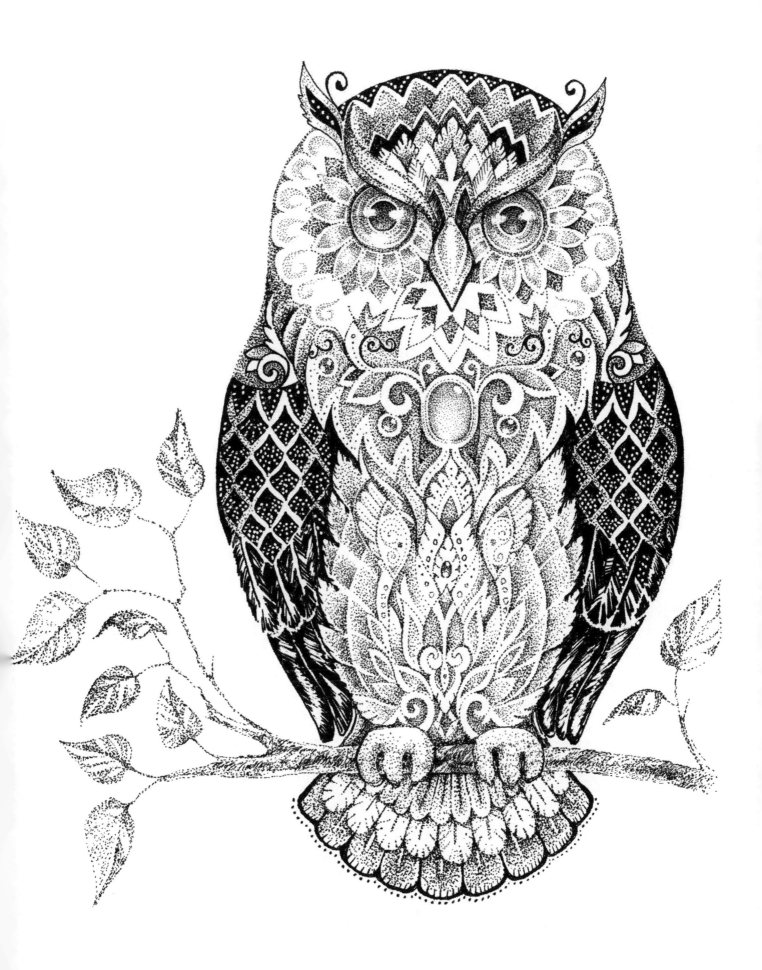

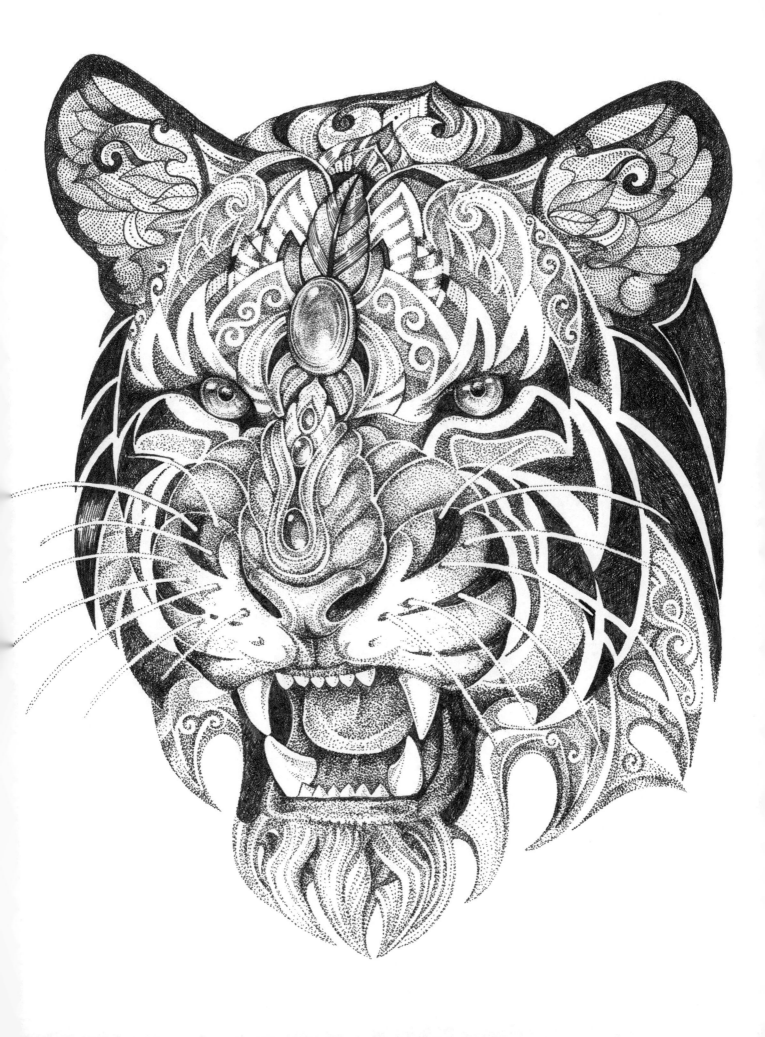

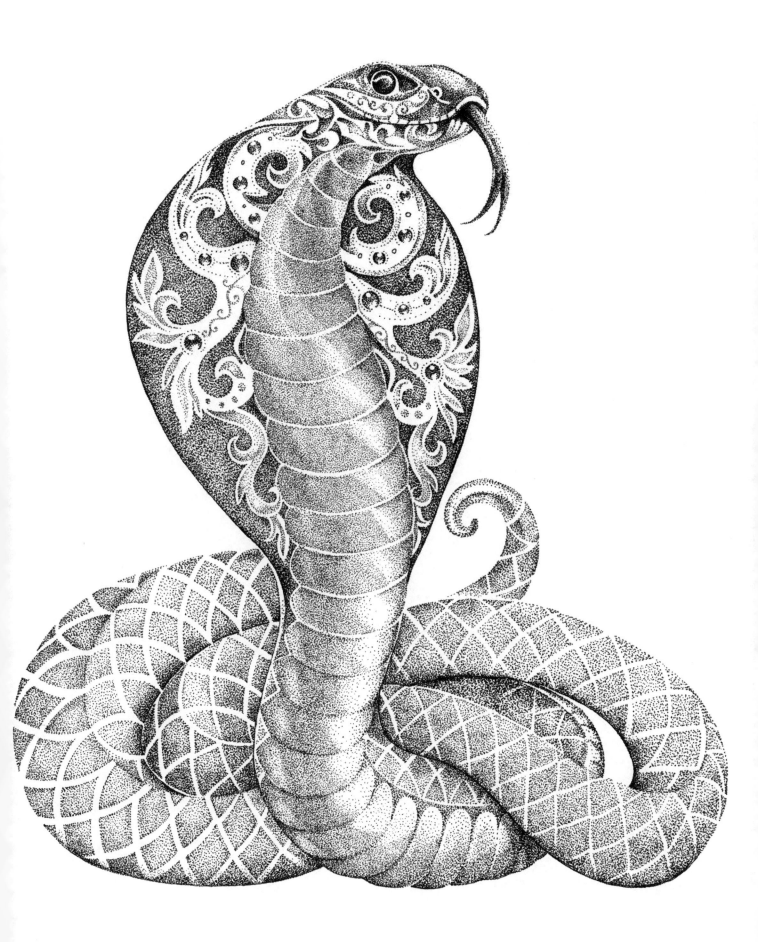

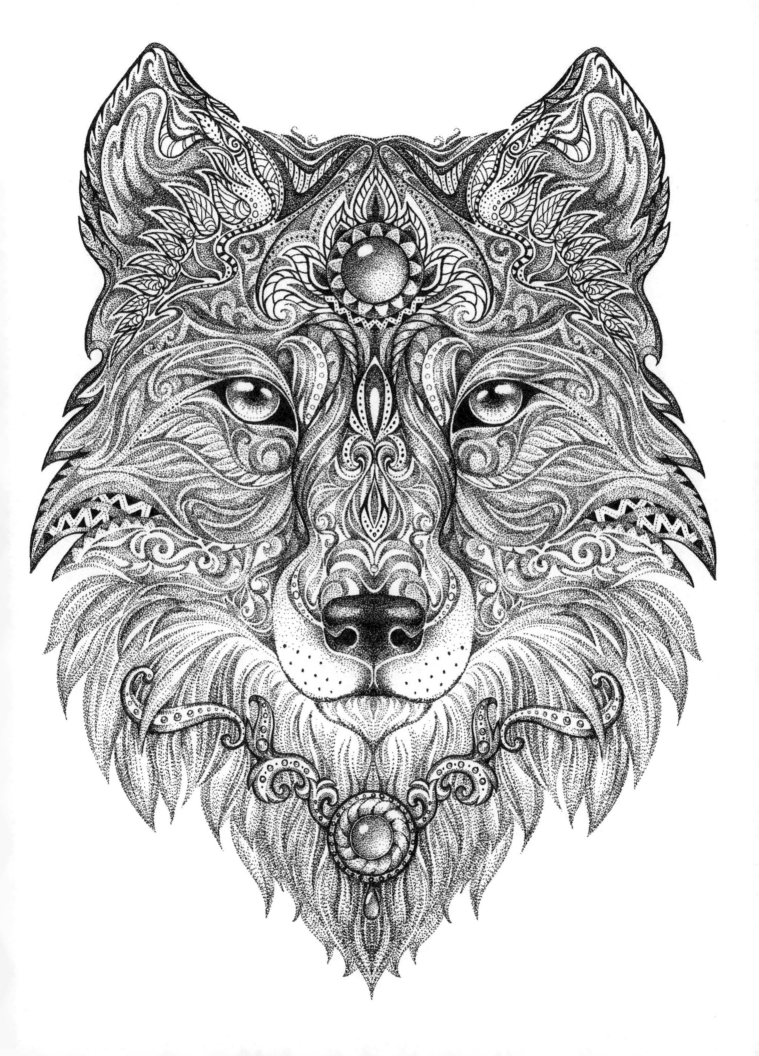

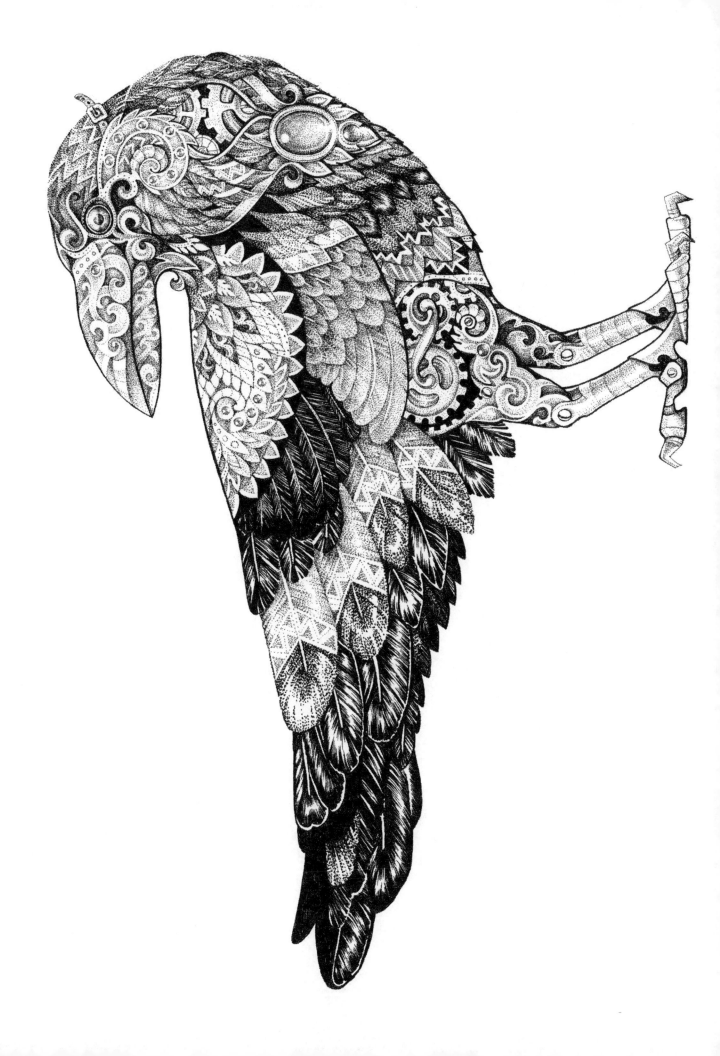

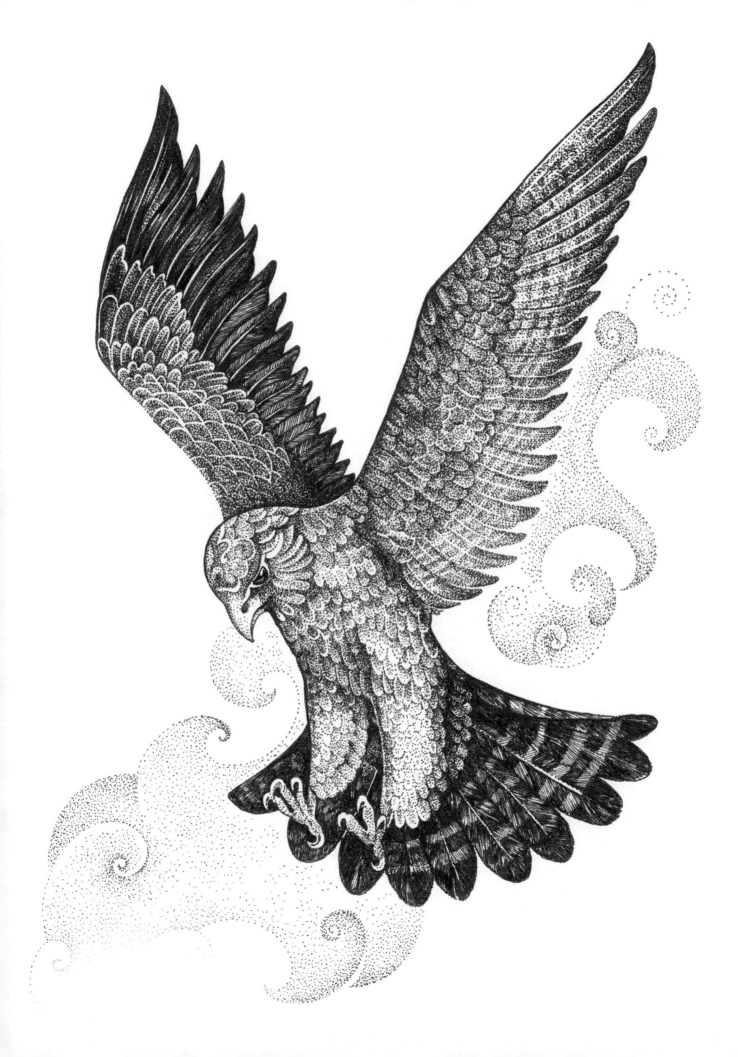

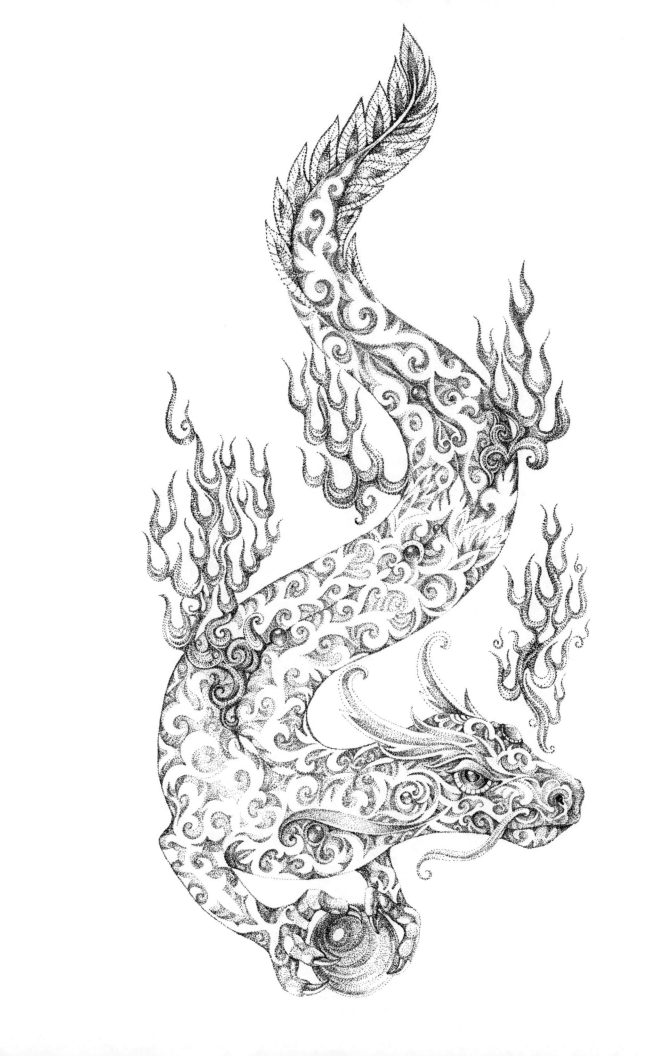

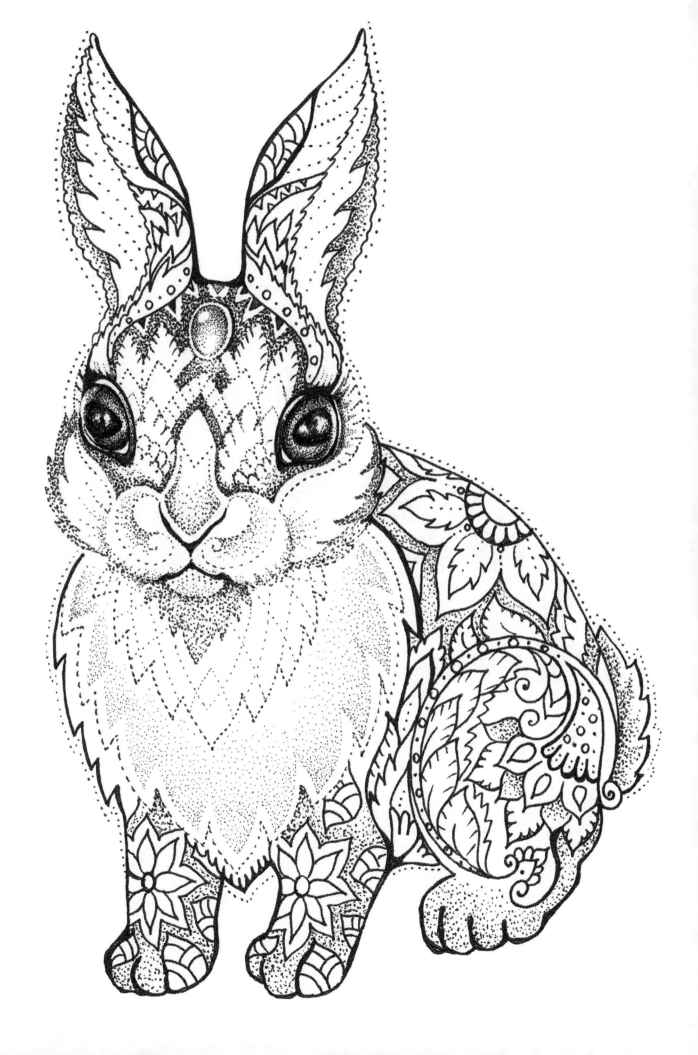

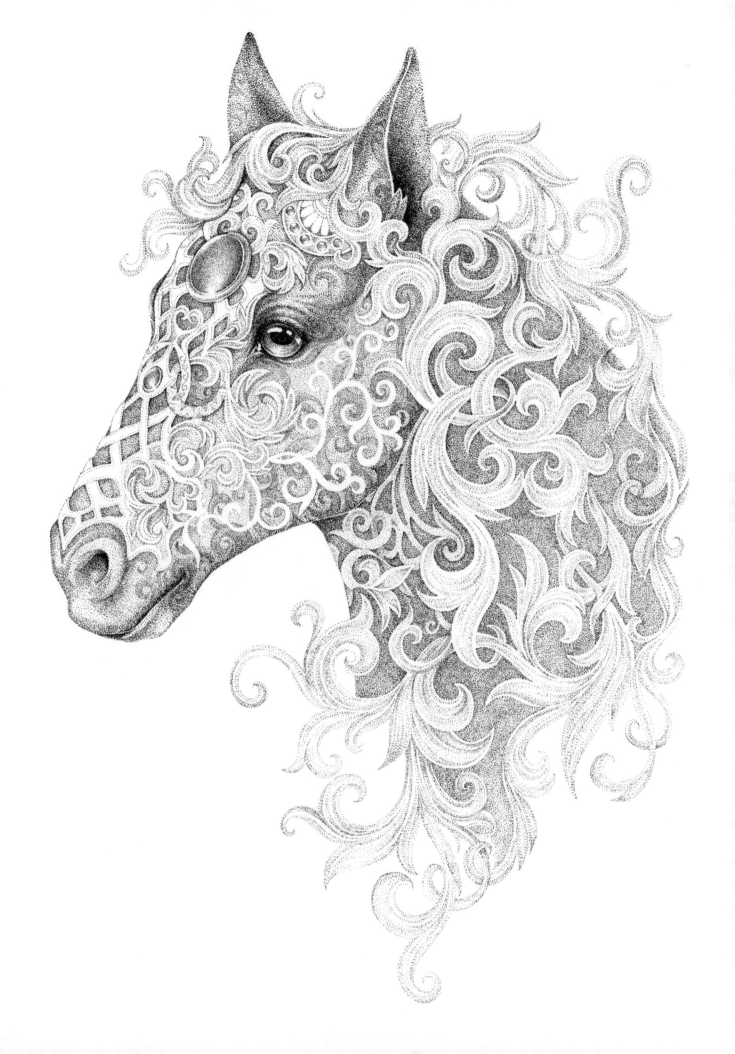

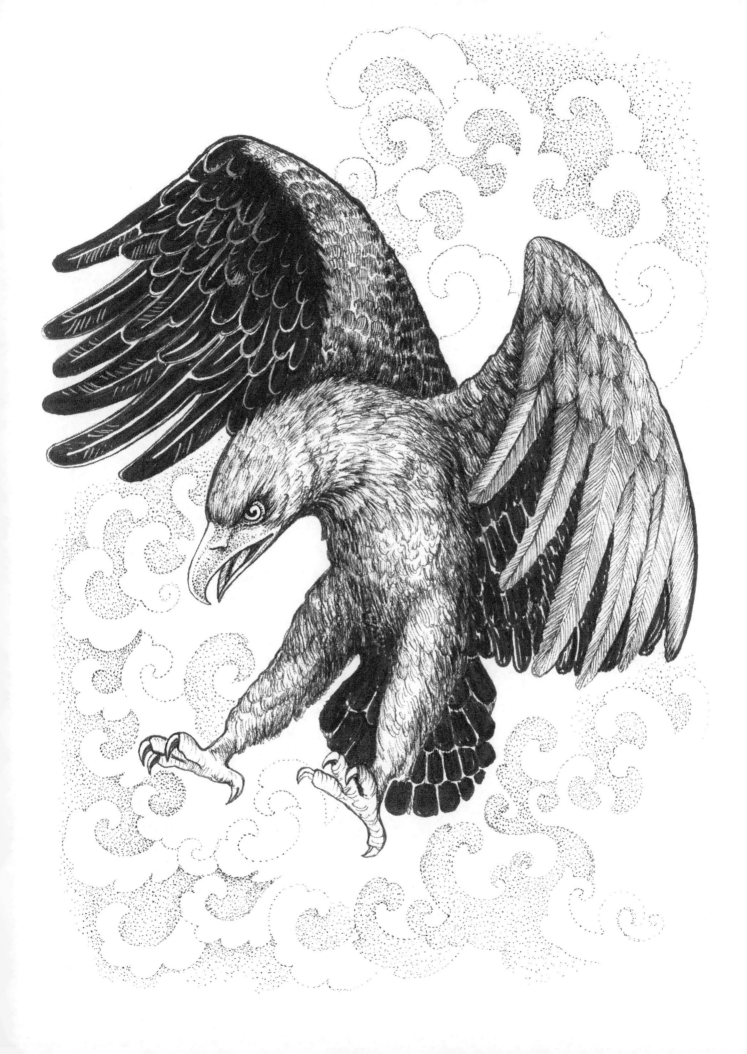

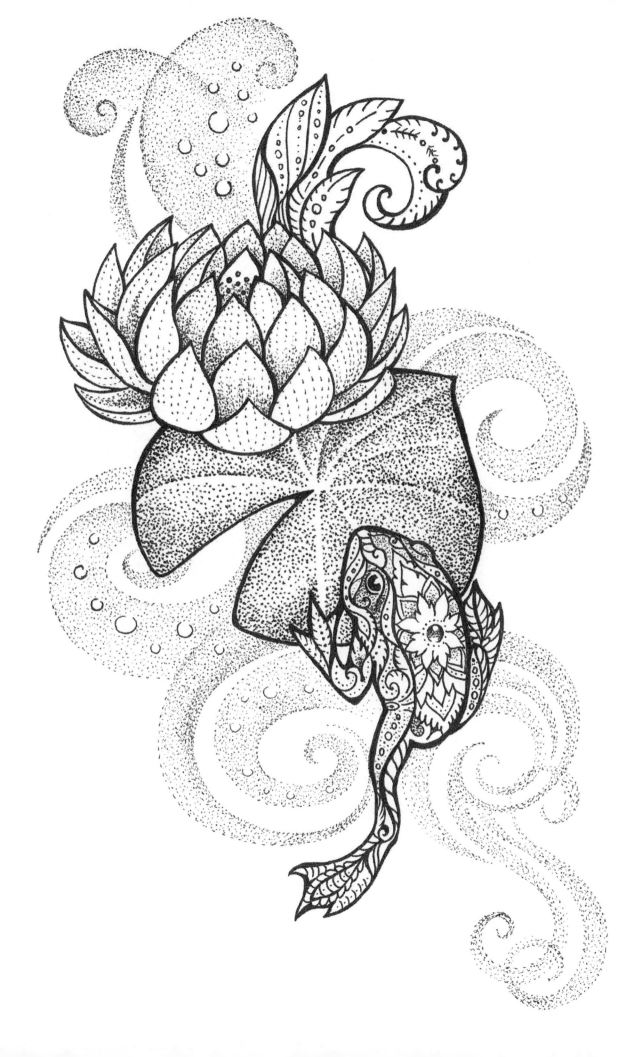

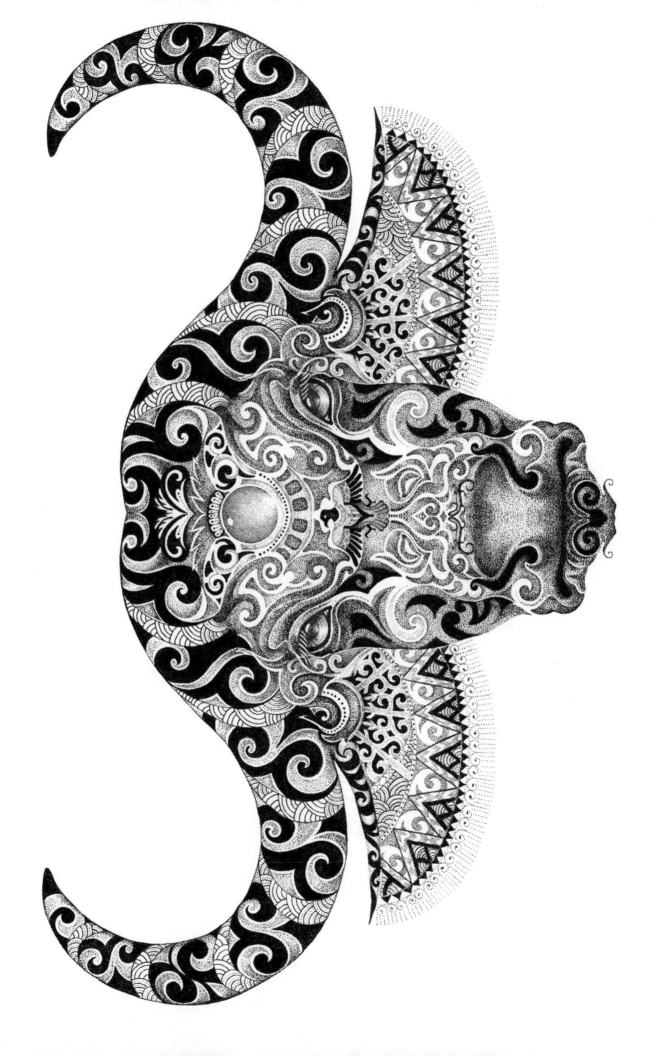

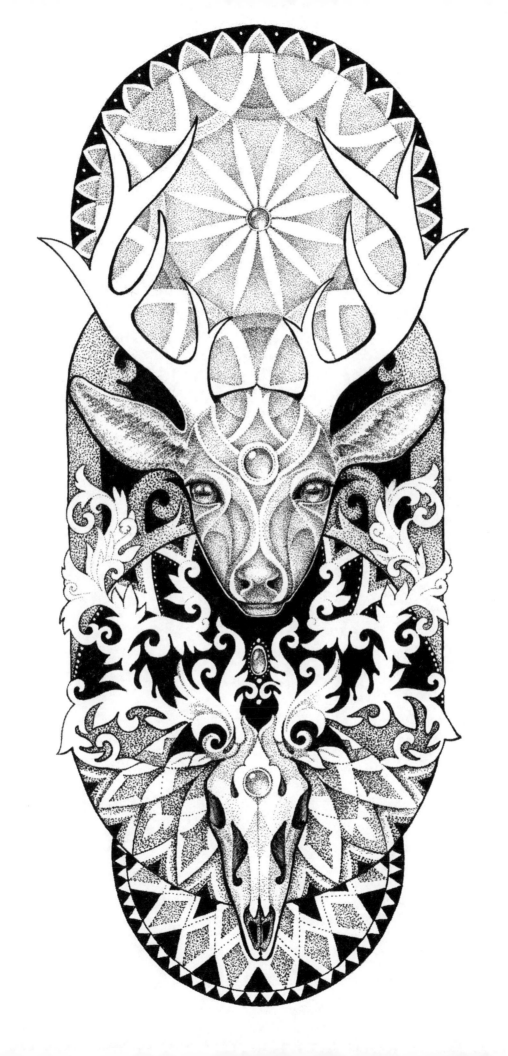

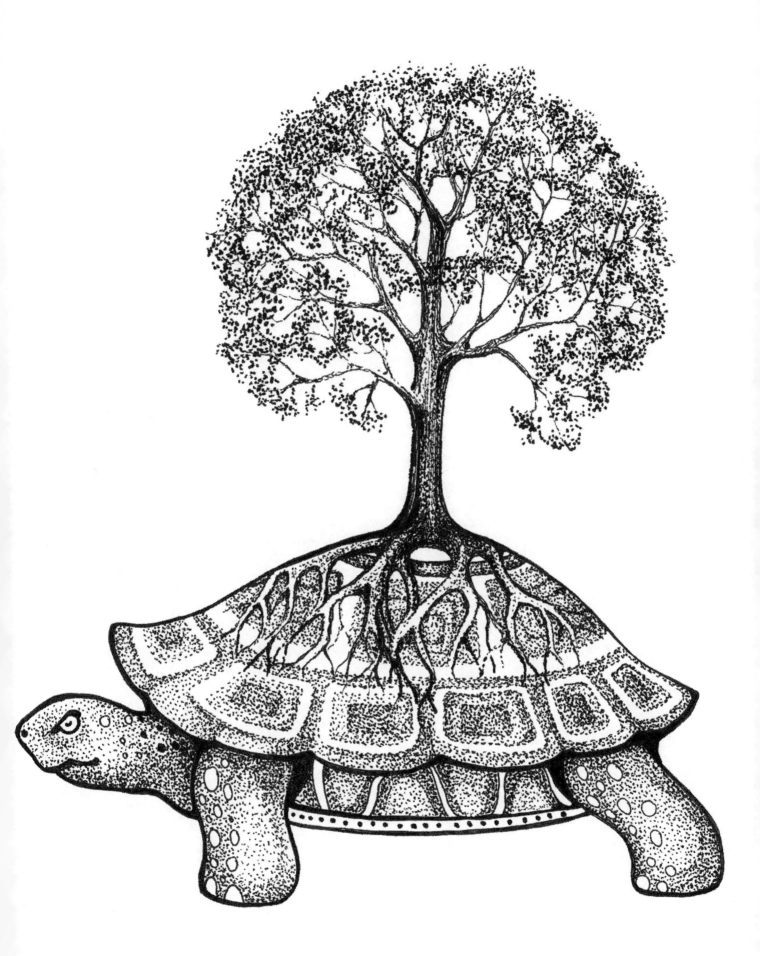

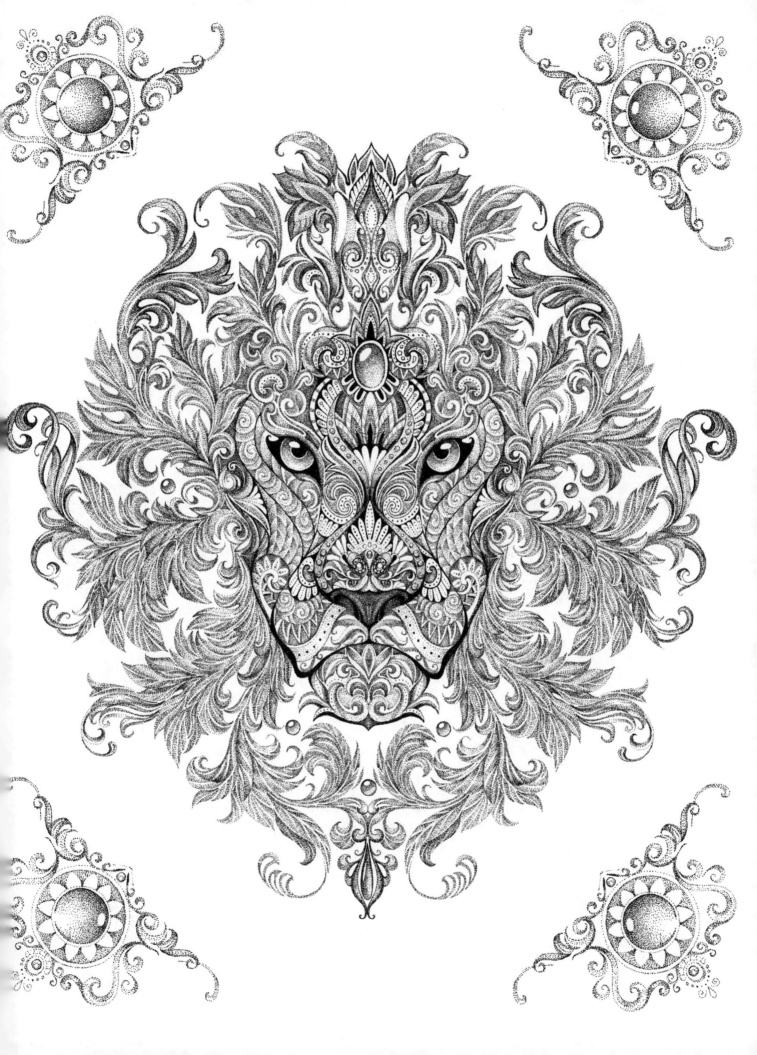

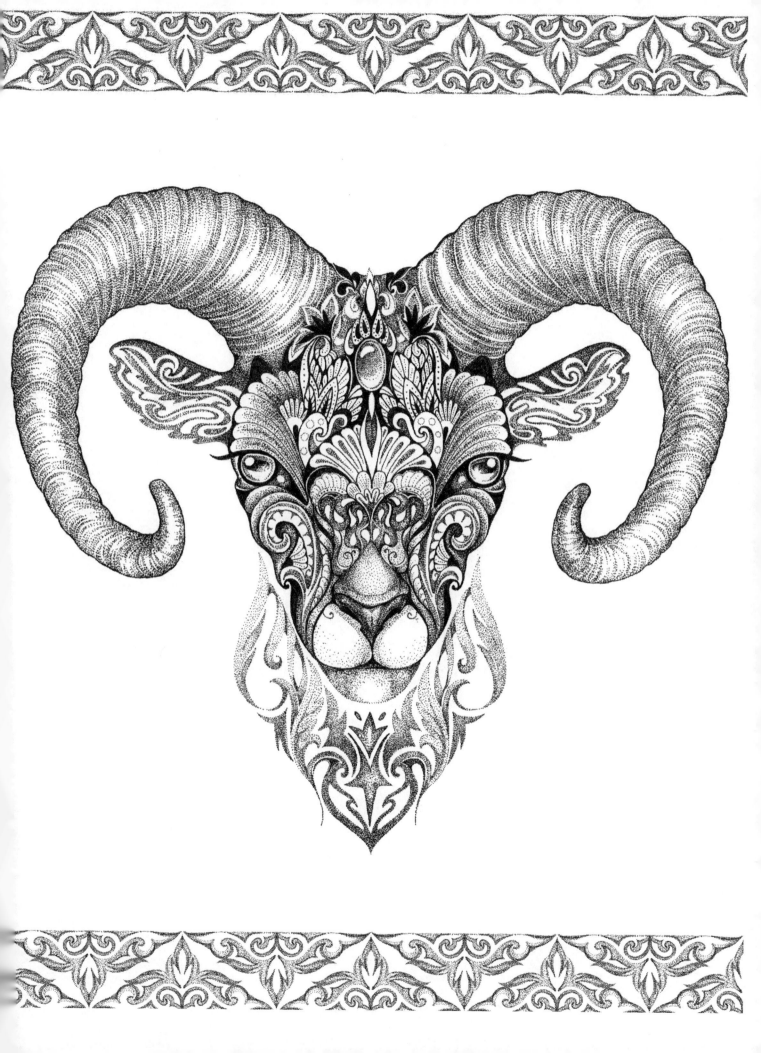

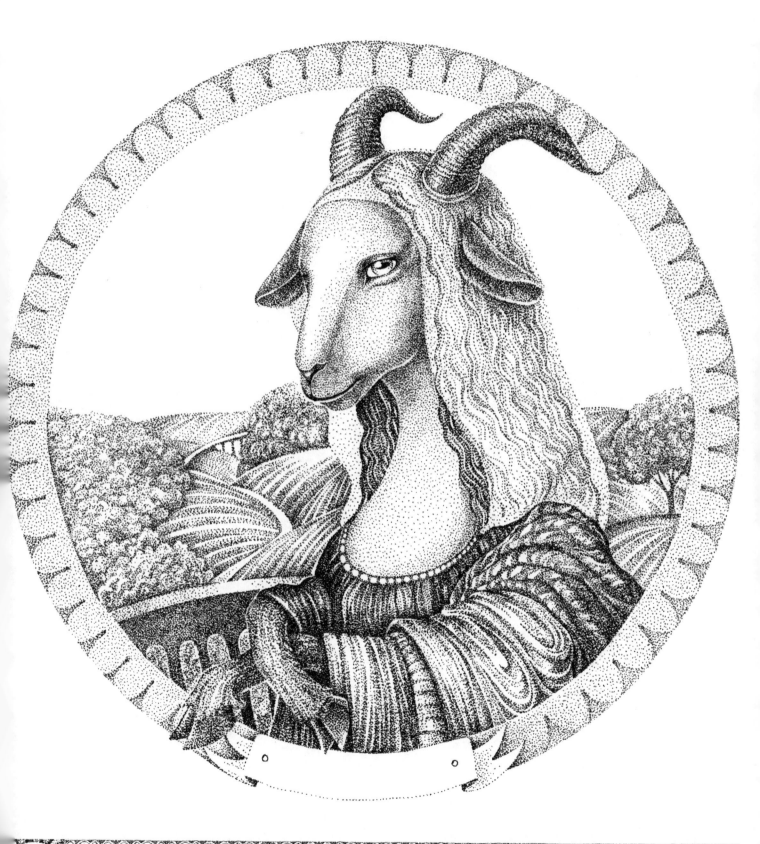

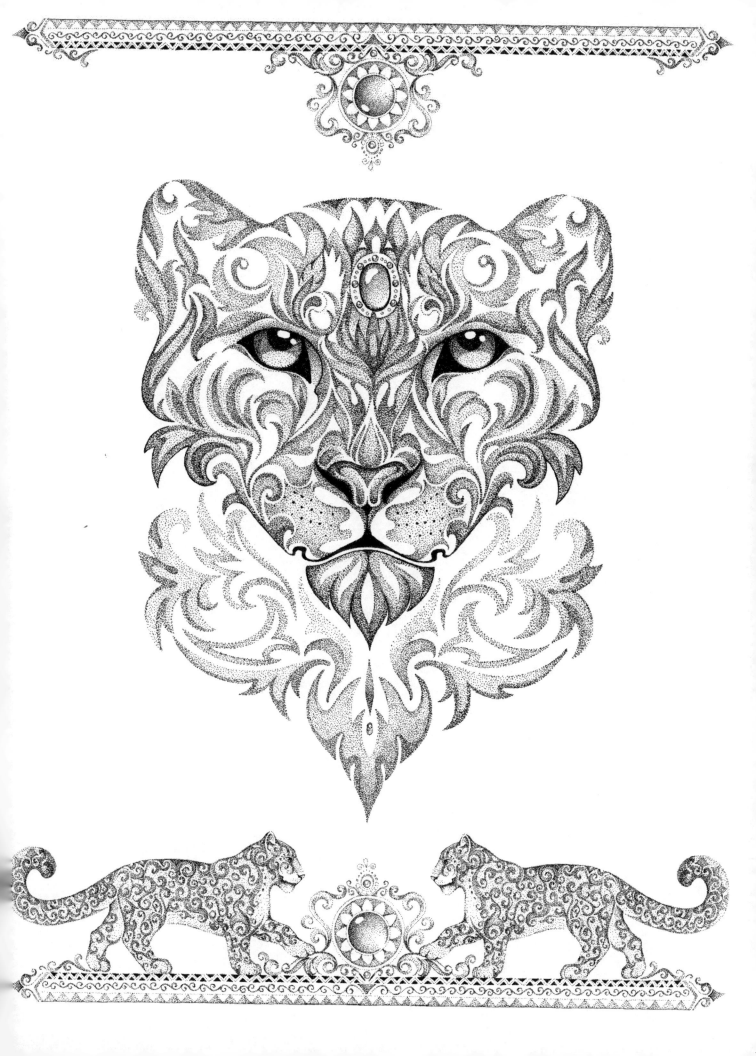

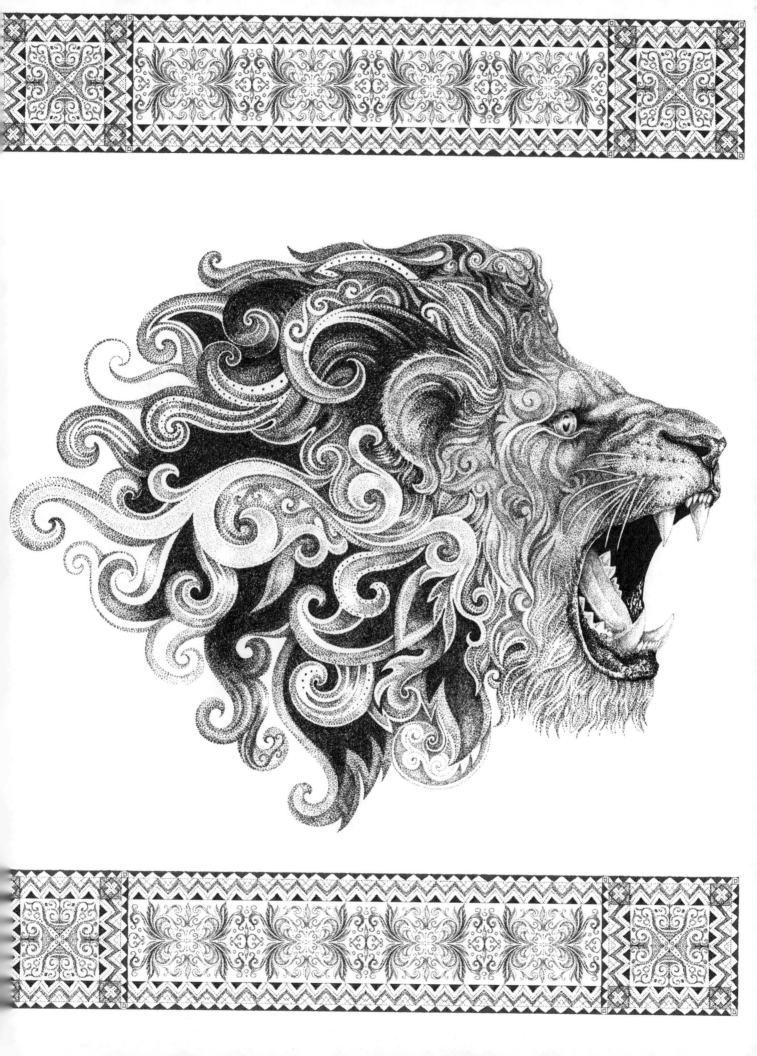

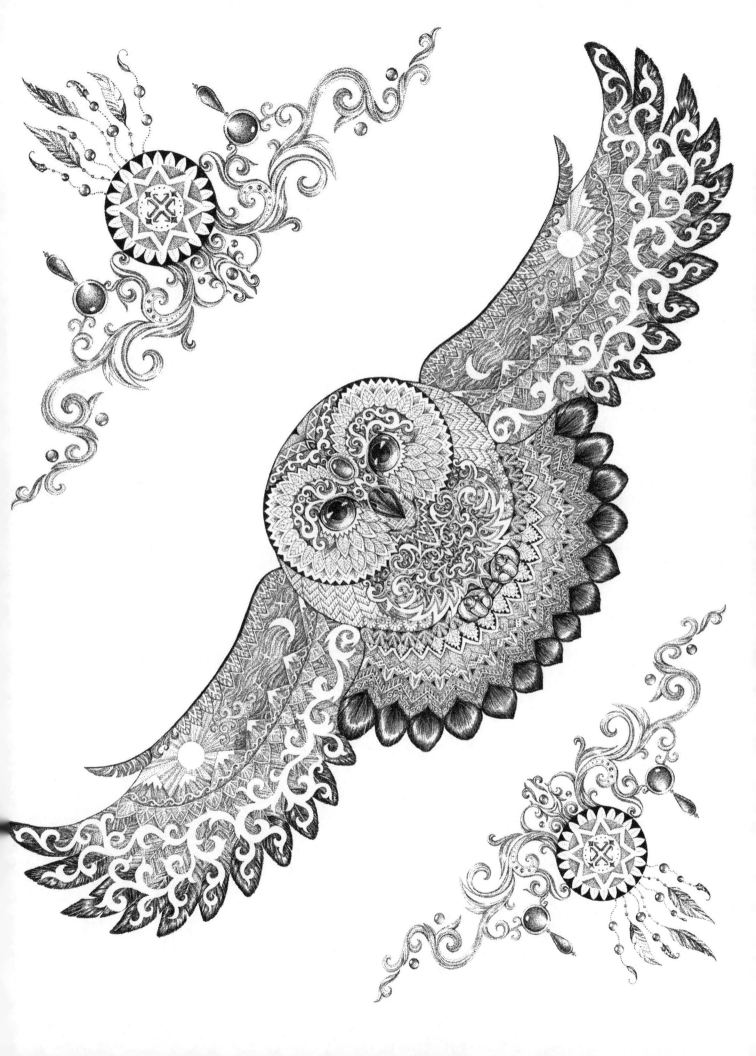

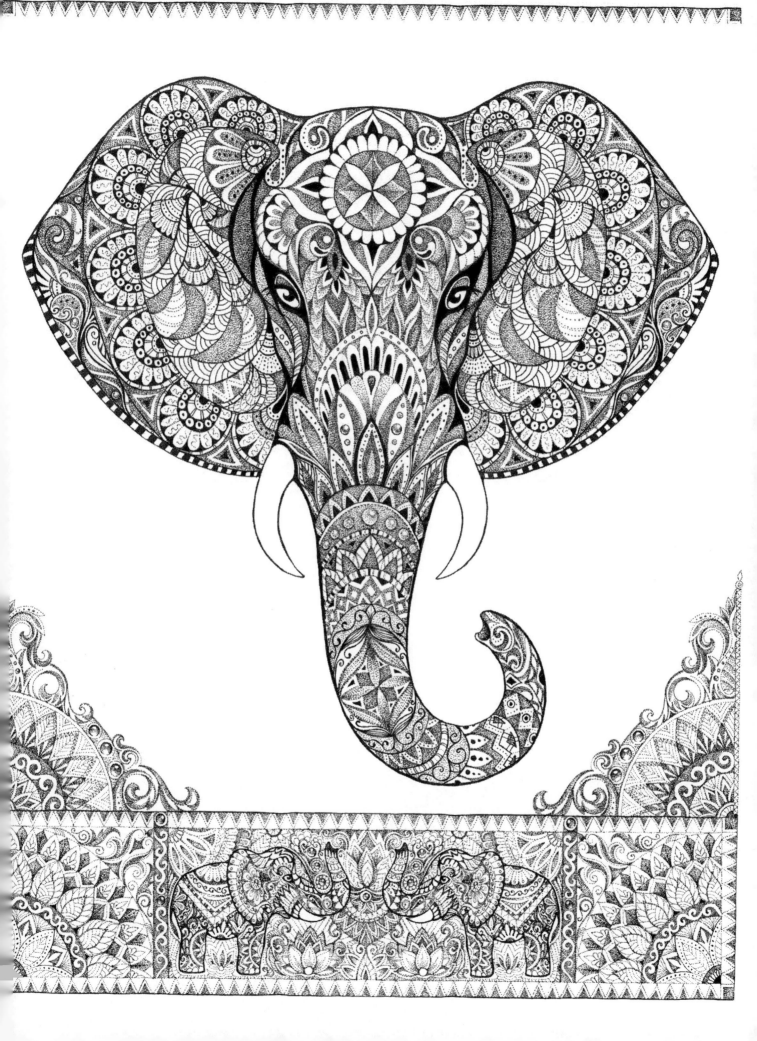

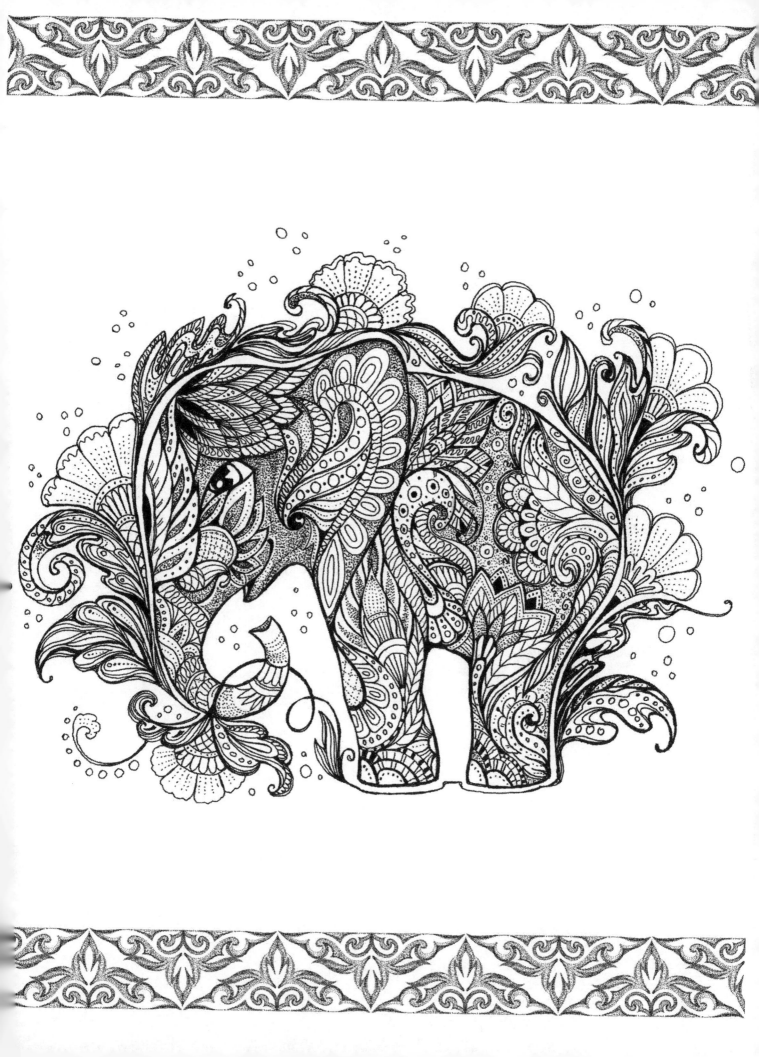

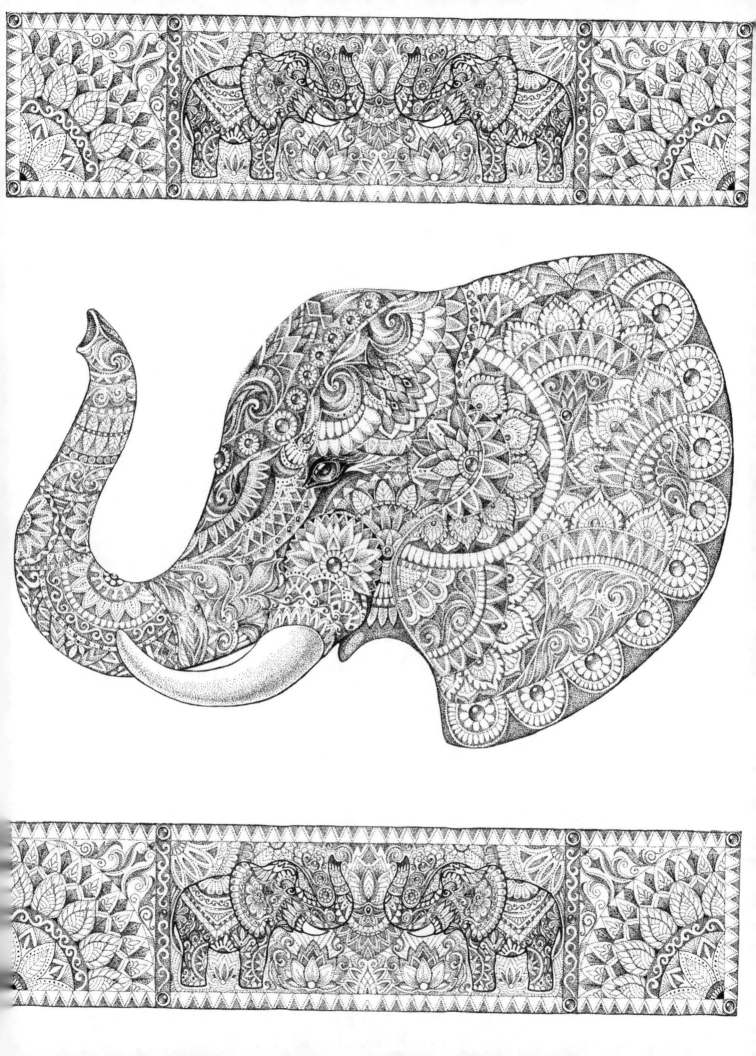

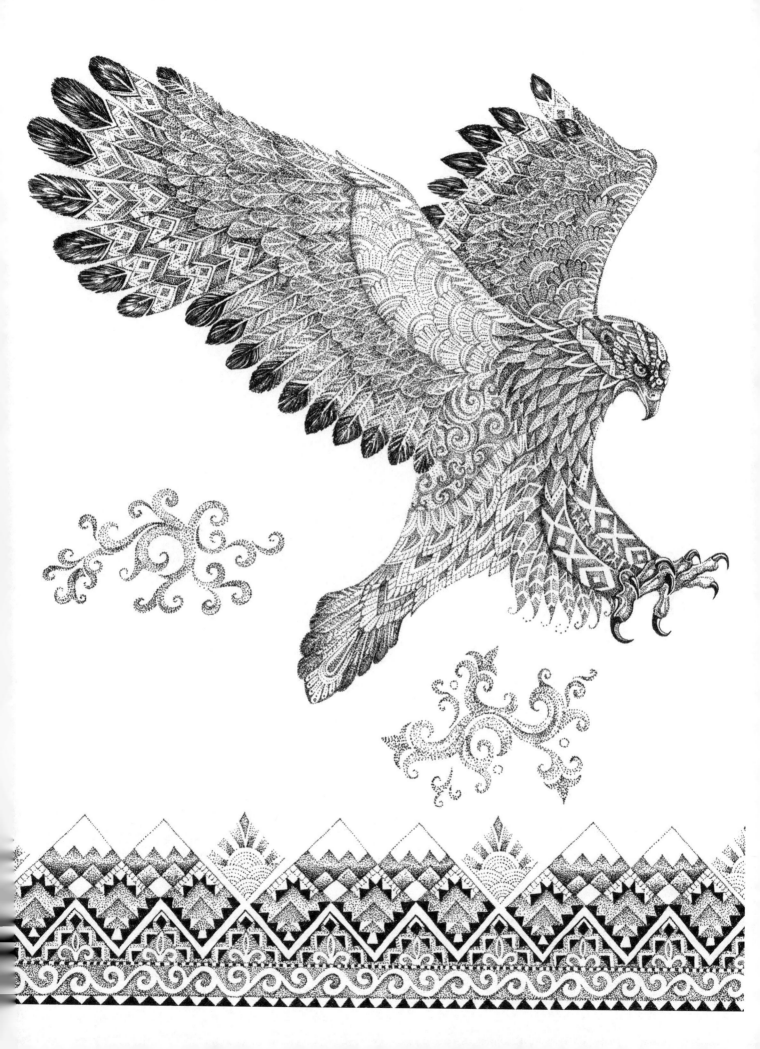

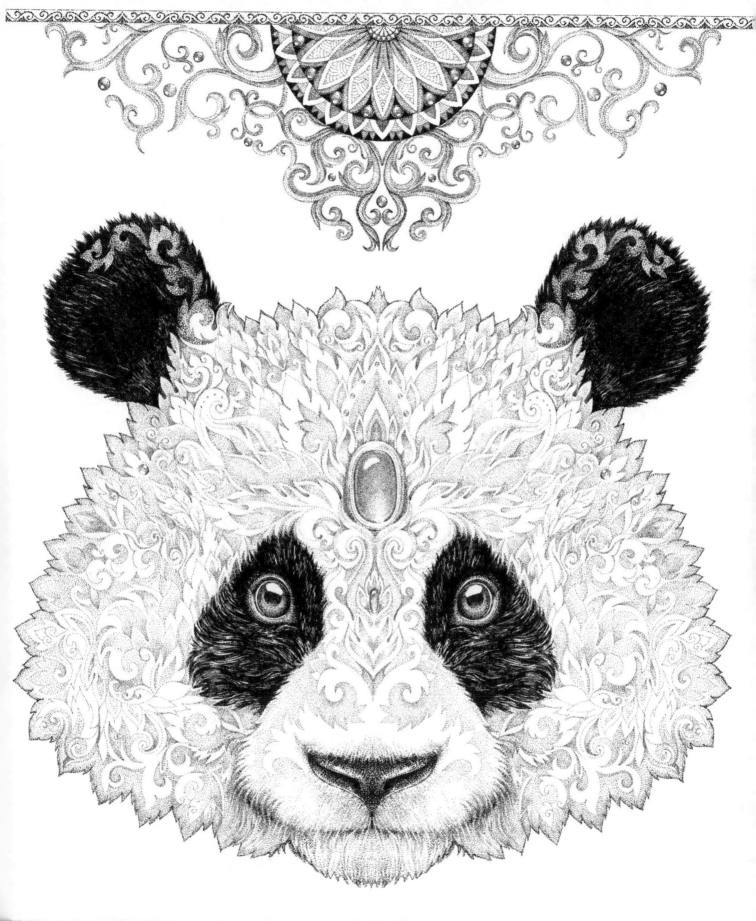

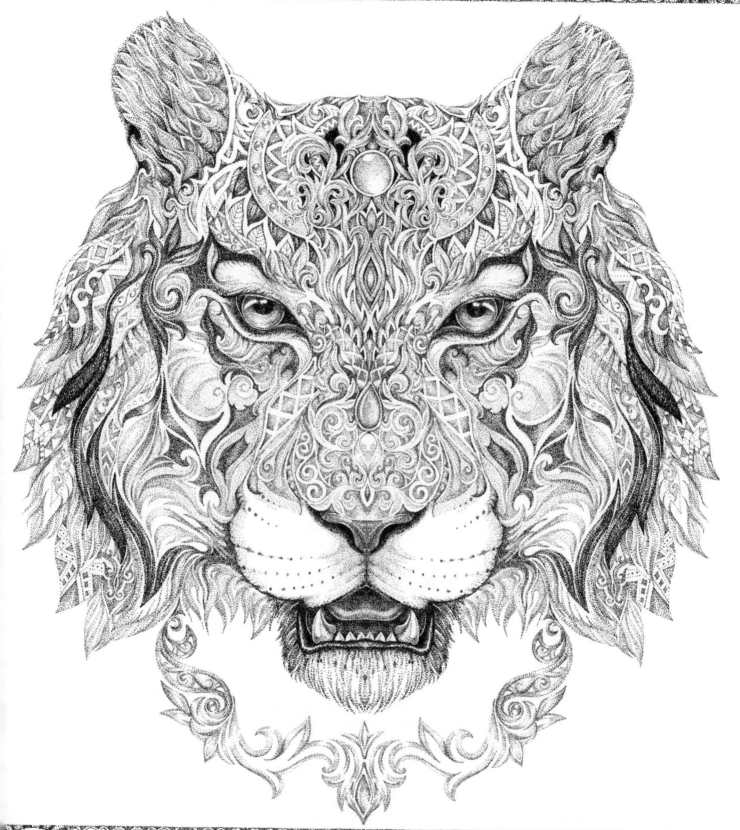

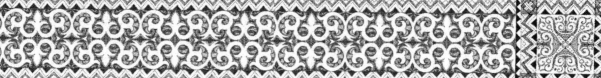

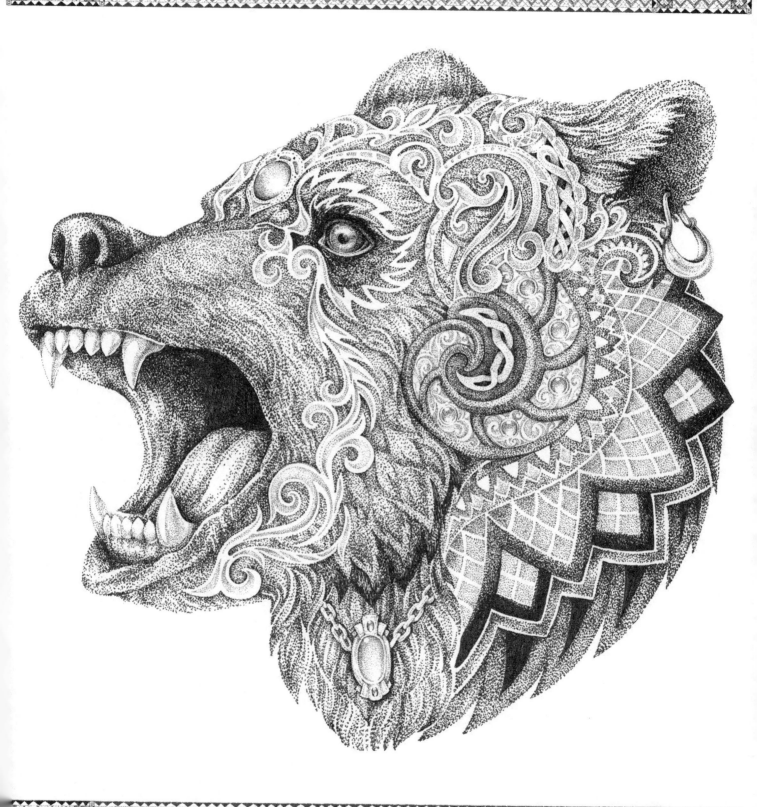

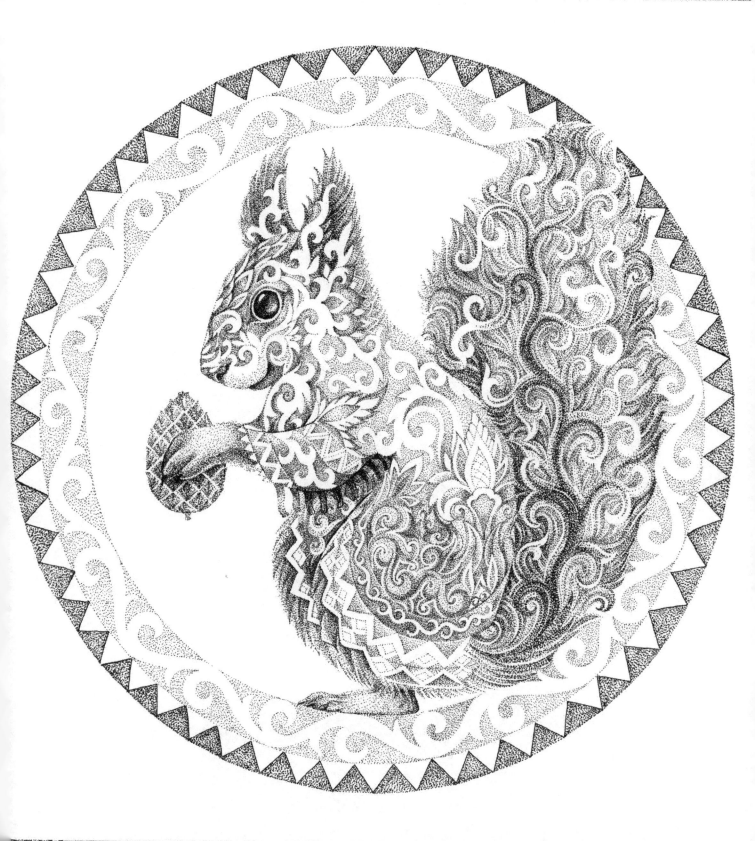

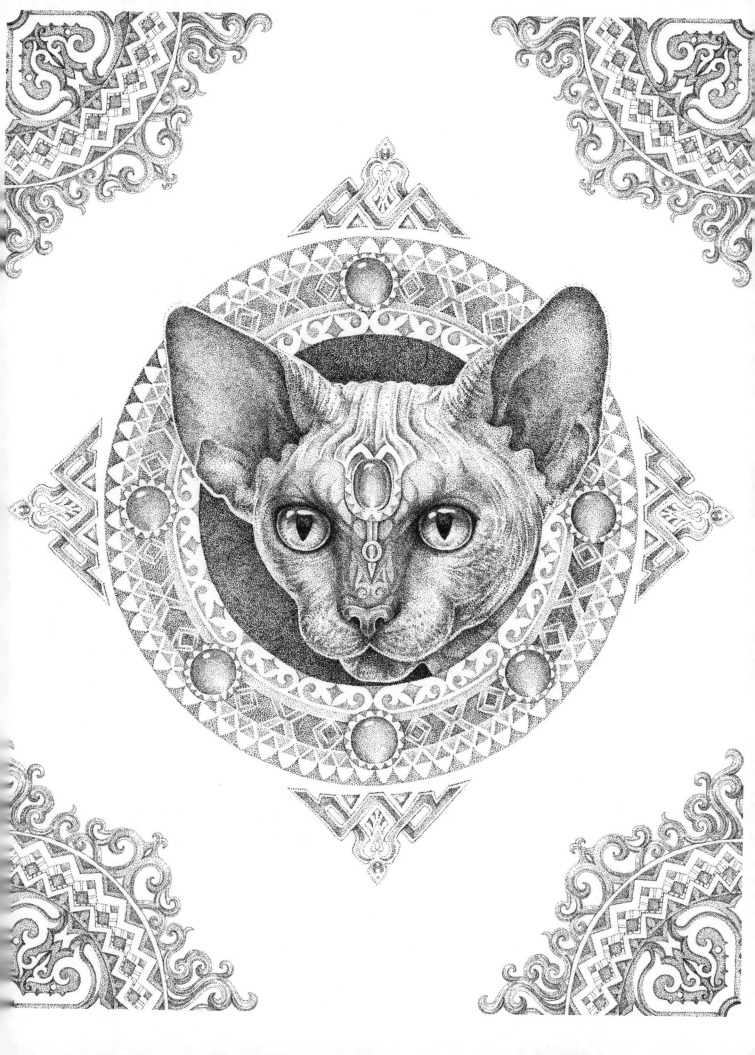

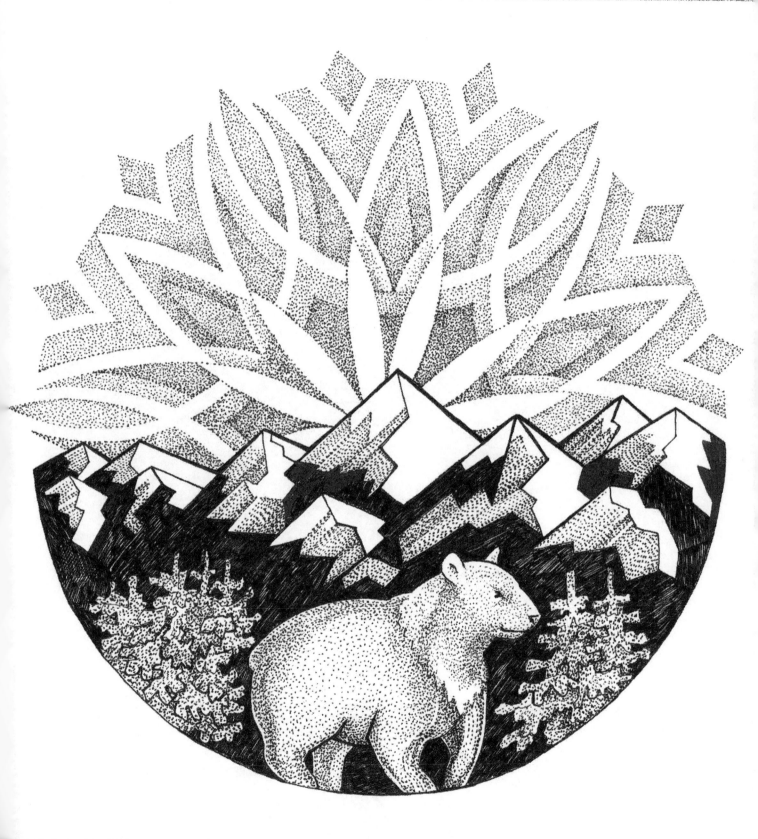

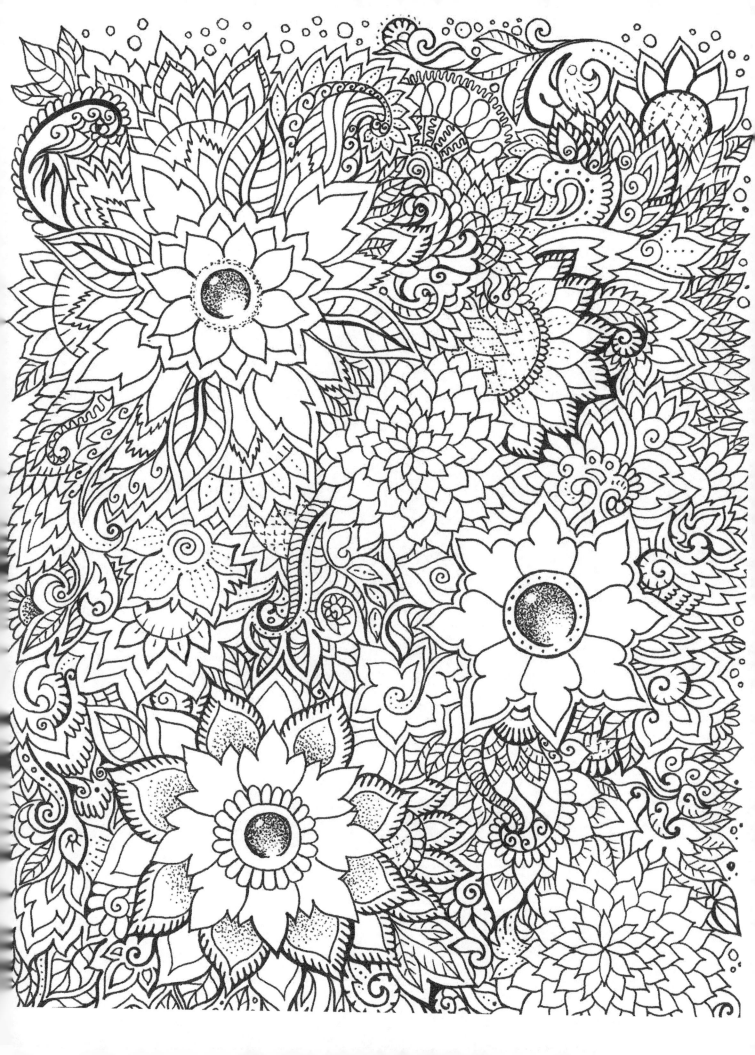

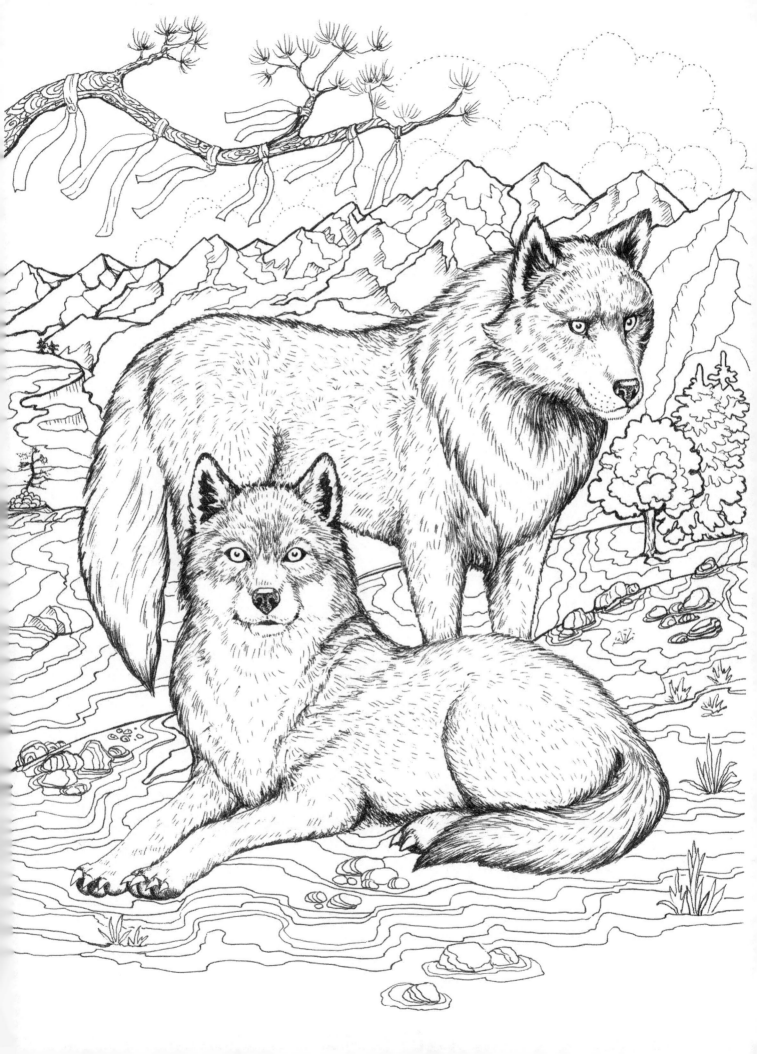

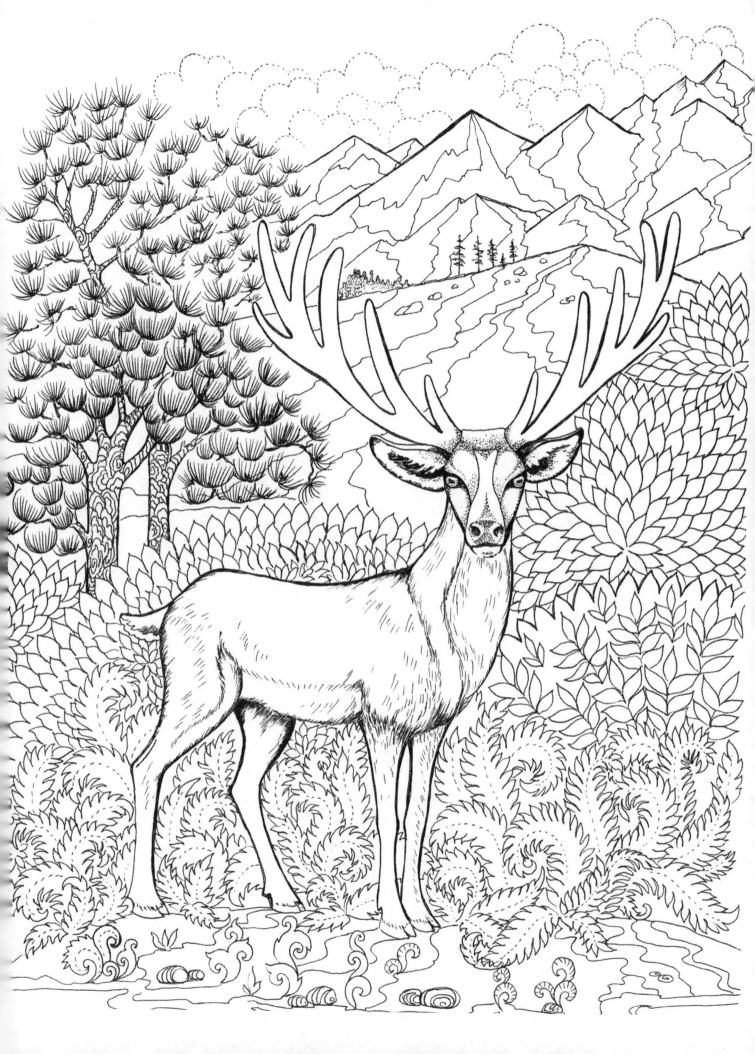

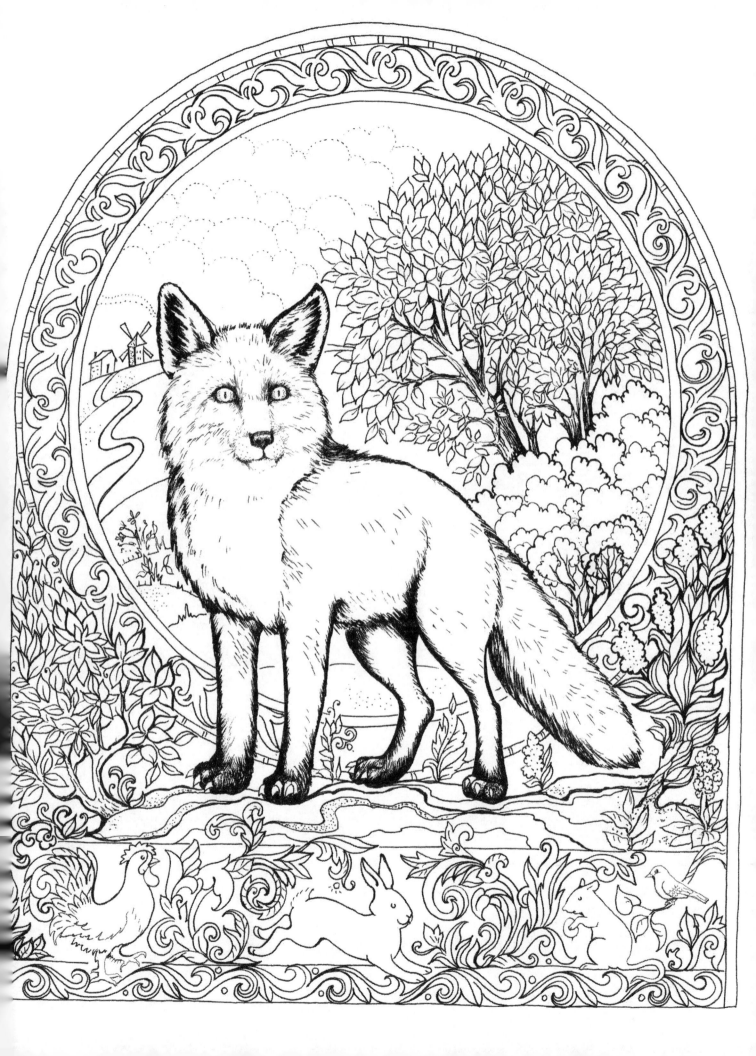

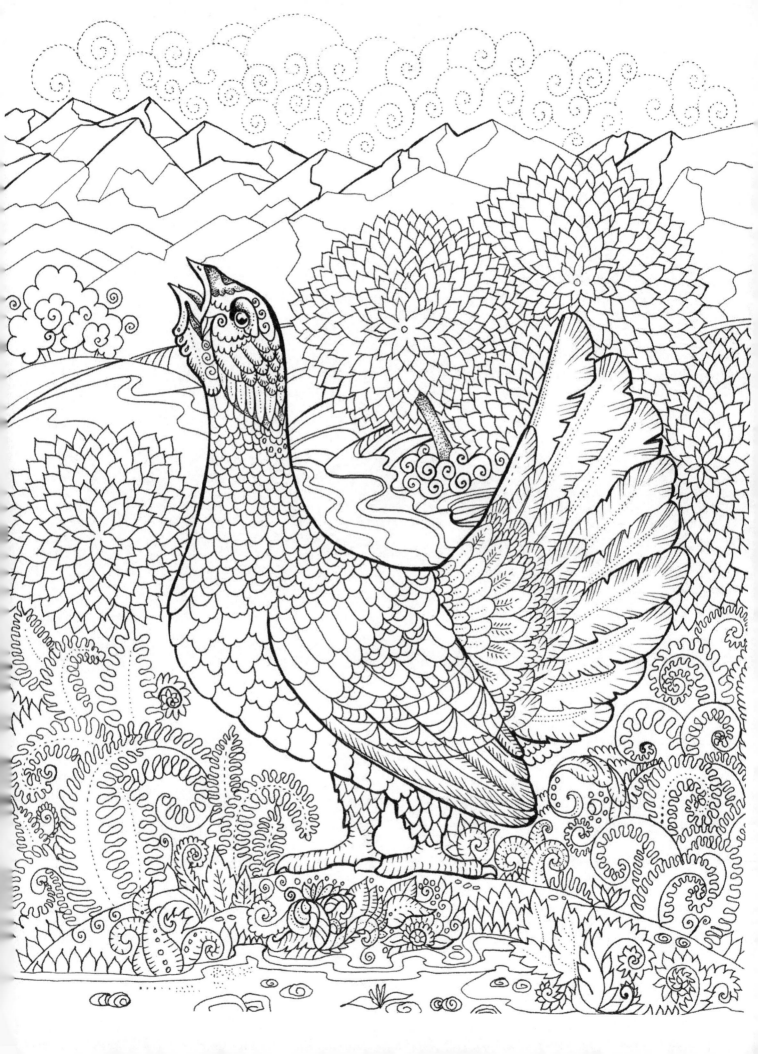

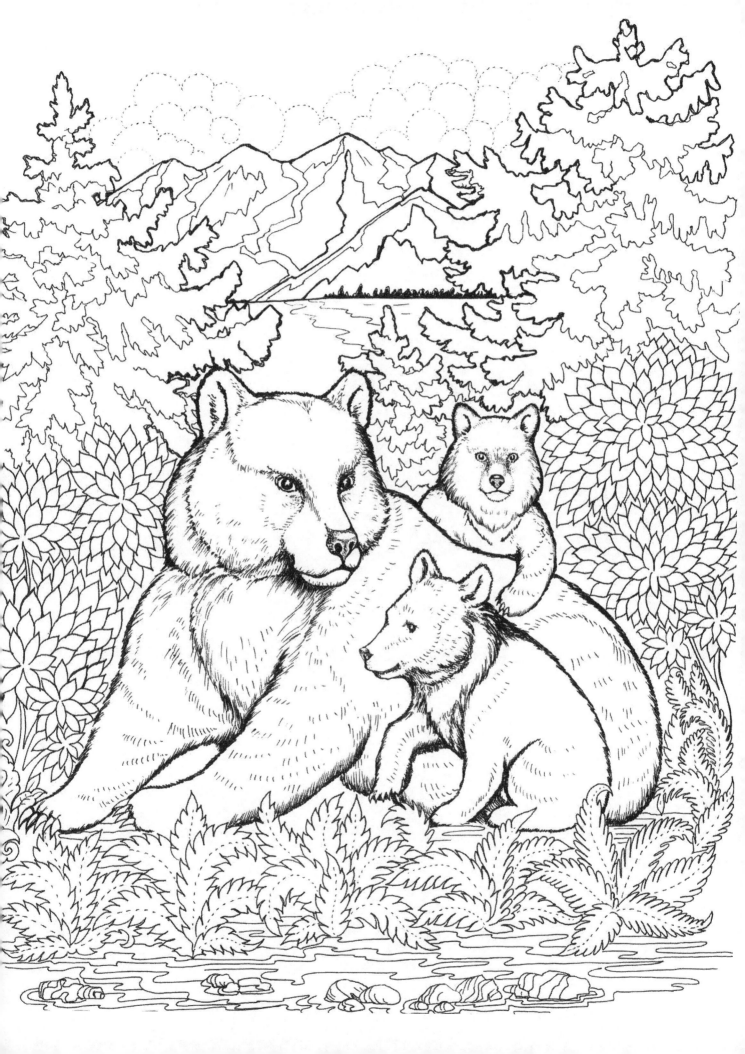

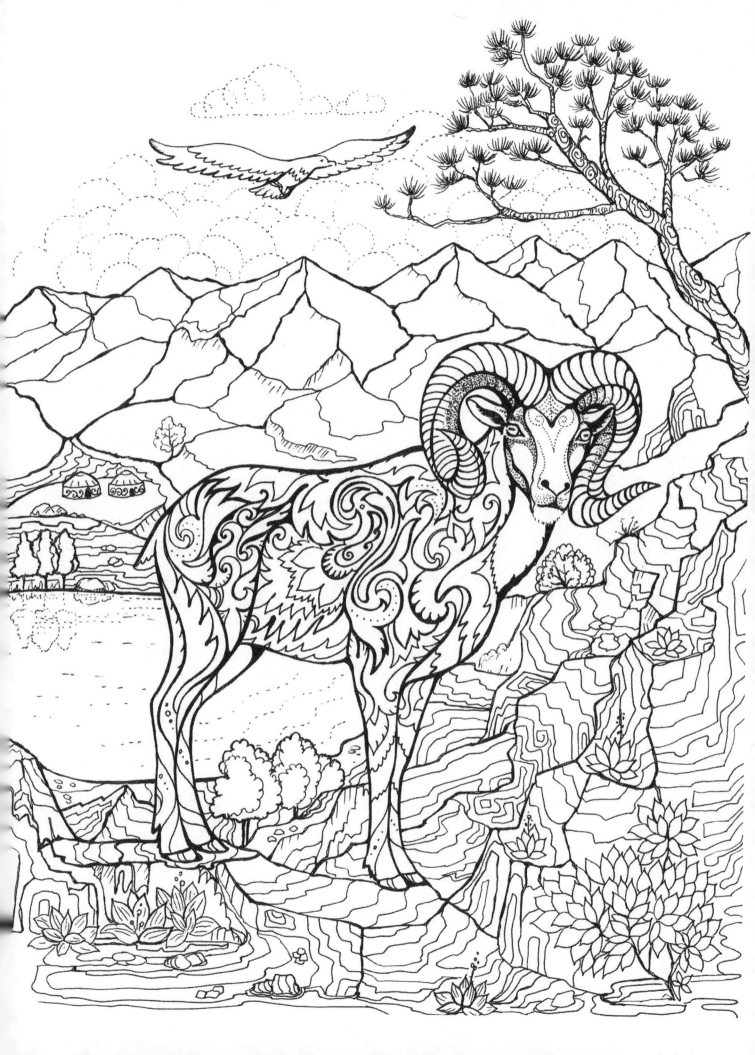

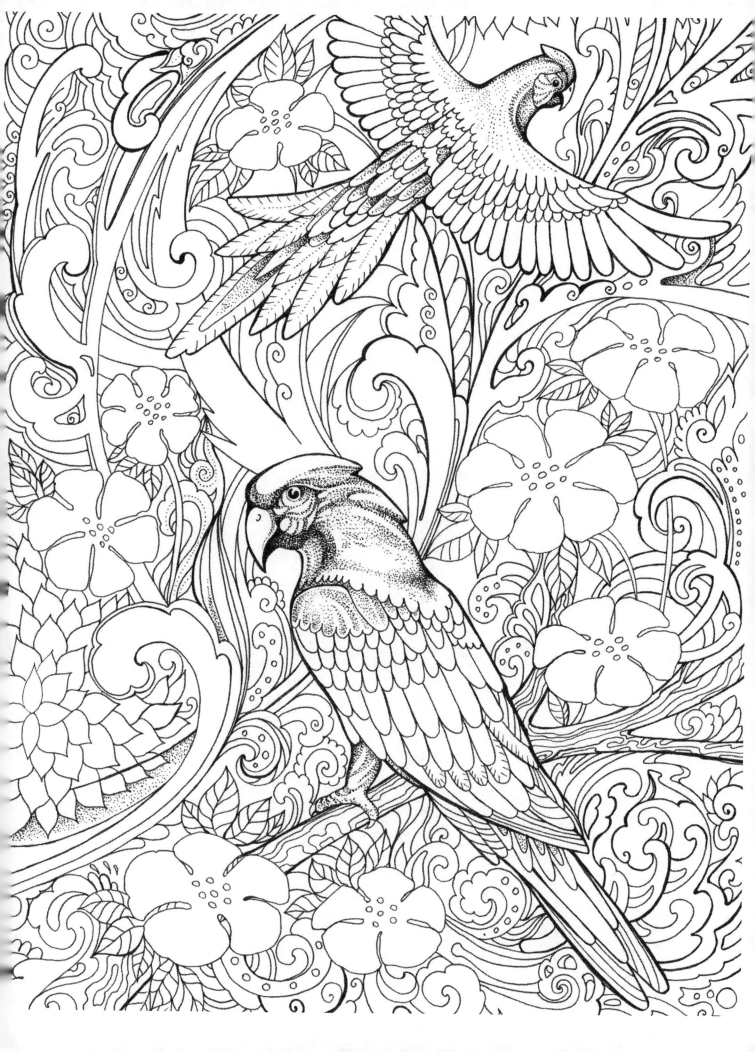

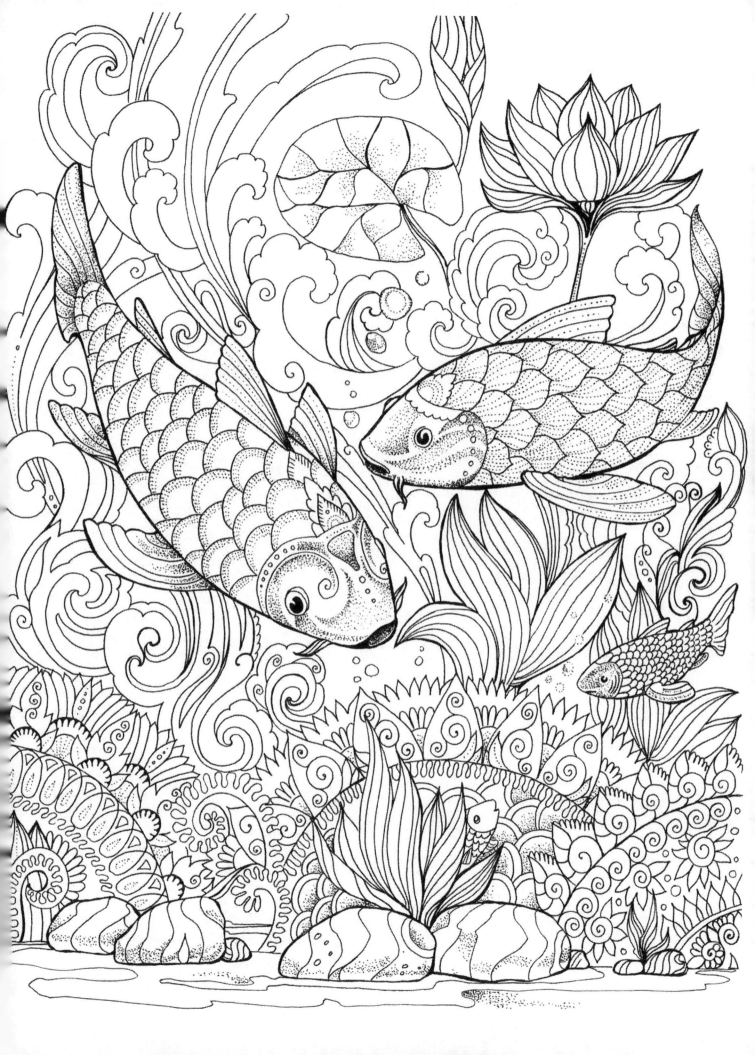

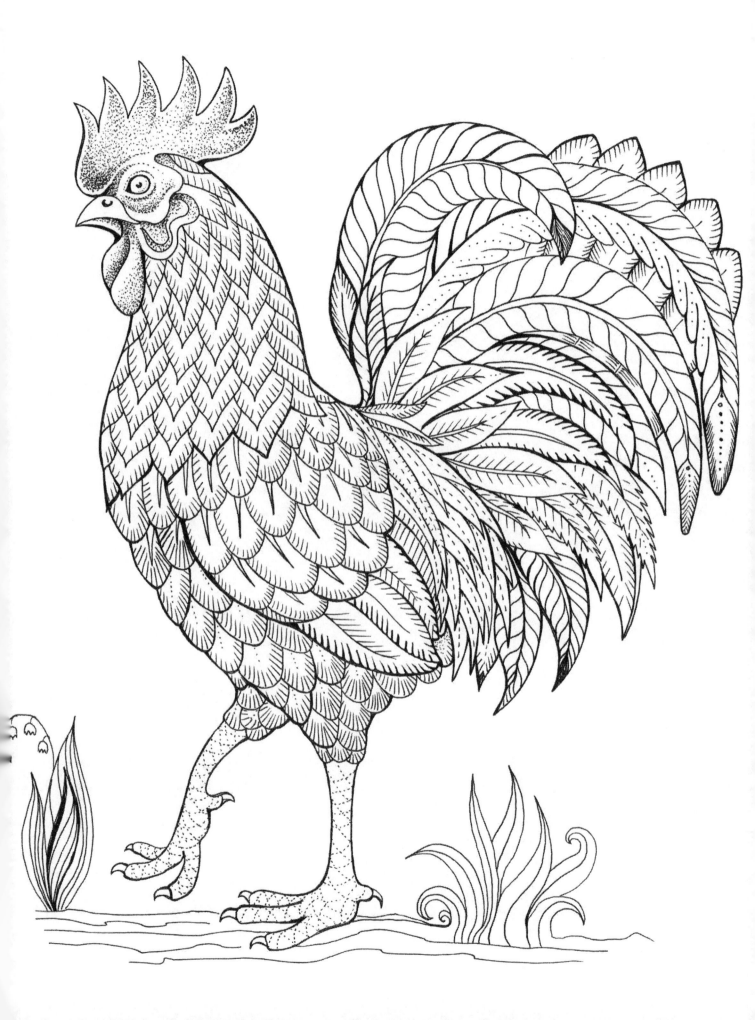

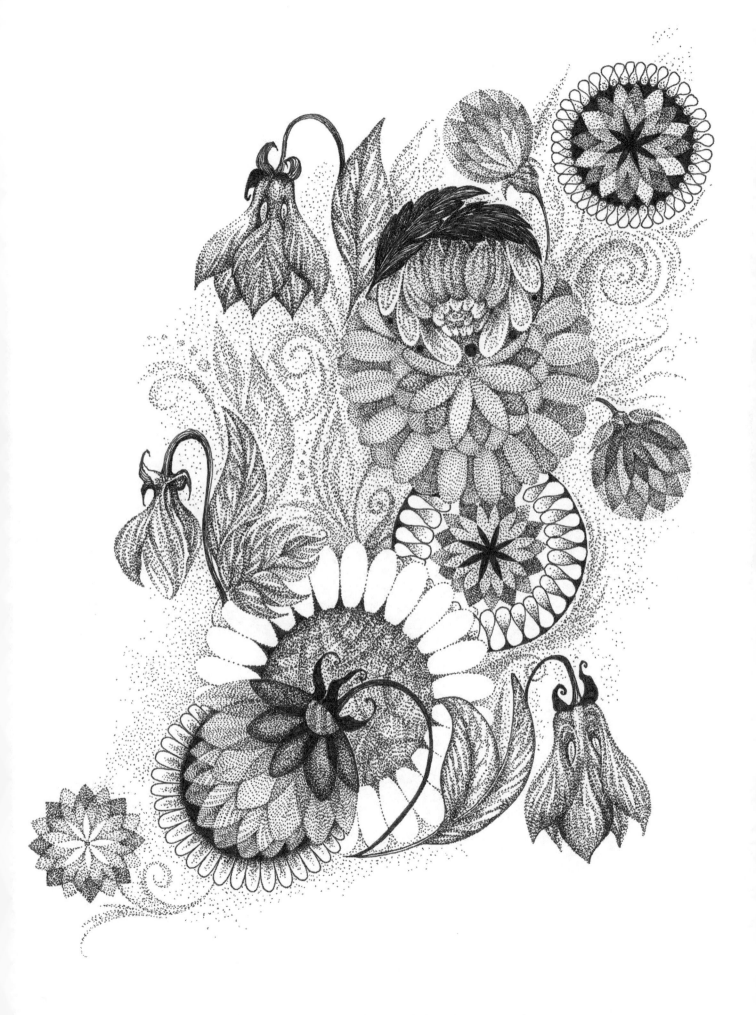

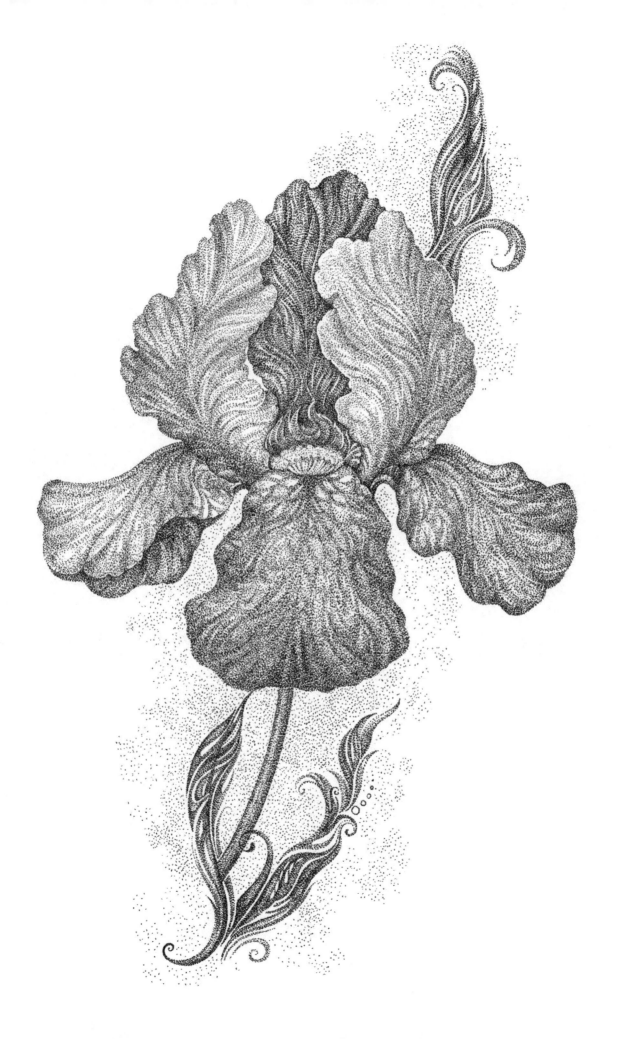

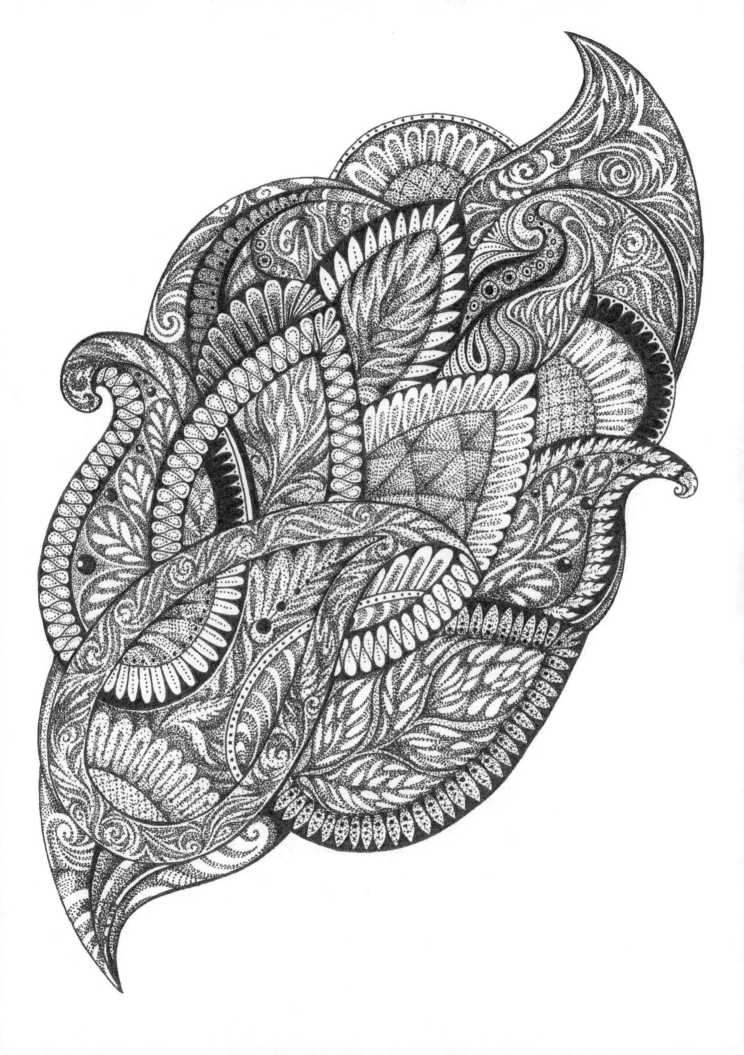

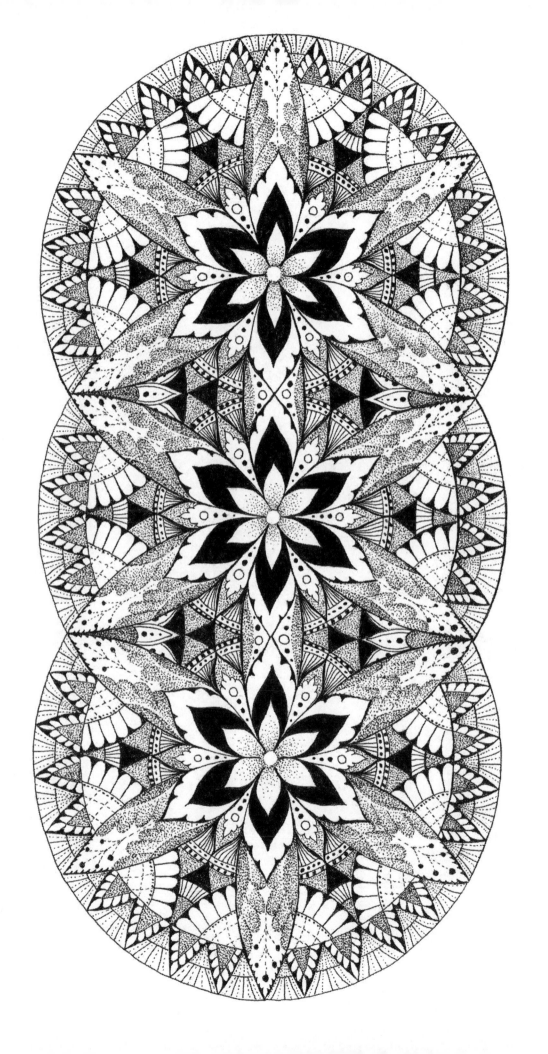

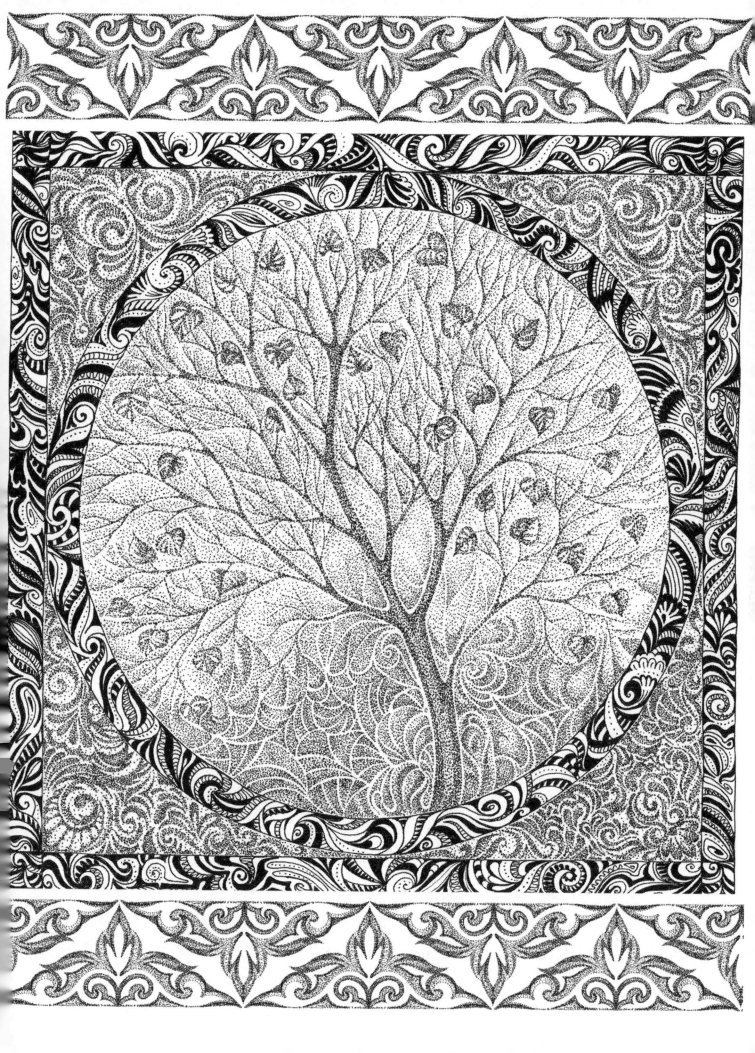

36236502R00058

Made in the USA
San Bernardino, CA
16 July 2016